Matthew Clark

Most Haunted

Hospitals and Asylums

Exorcisms and Possessions

A Scary Journey in the Most Haunted Hospitals and Asylums and in the Most Famous True Stories of Exorcisms and Demonic Possessions

Copyright © 2021 publishing.

All rights reserved.

Author: Matthew Clark

No part of this publication may be reproduced, distributed or transmitted in any form or by any means, including photocopying recording or other electronic or mechanical methods or by any information storage and retrieval system without the prior written permission of the publisher, except in the case of brief quotation embodies in critical reviews and certain other non-commercial uses permitted by copyright law.

Table of Contents

BOOK 1: Most Haunted Hospitals and Asylums

Introduction 6
1. Ararat Lunatic Asylum 9
2. Beechworth Lunatic Asylum 17
3. Nummela Sanatorium 27
4. Old Changi Hospital 38
5. Gonjiam Psychiatric Hospital 44
6. Waverly Hills Sanatorium, Louisville, Ky 56
7. Hospital For Mental Illness In Whittingham 67
8. Lunatic Asylum In Trans-Allegheny 76
9. Lier Sykehus Psychiatric Hospital 84
10. Royal Hope Hospital 91
11. The Northville State Hospital 98
Conclusion 103

BOOK 2: Most Haunted Exorcisms and Possessions

Introduction 107
1. The Exorcism of Anneliese Michel 109

2. The Exorcism of Anna Ecklund 118
3. The Exorcism of Roland Doe 125
4. David Berkowitz, Son of Sam Demonic Possession..... 131
5. Carolyn Perron and the Perron Family 140
6. The Defeo Family (Amityville Horror) 149
7. Exorcism of Michael Taylor 157
8. Exorcism of Clara Germana Cele 162
9. The Smurl's Poltergeist 170
10. The Tanacu Exorcism of Maricica Irina Cornici 178
11. Nicole Aubrey's Possession 185
12. Elizabeth Knapp (The Groton Witch) 194
Conclusion: 199

Introduction

Are you looking for spooky, eerie things to do for Halloween? Try visiting a haunted hospital or asylum. Millions of people worldwide are entranced by the various tales of curses, ghosts, and other paranormal phenomena. What better place to experience all the dark, eerie, and terrifying spirits of the afterlife than a former psychiatric hospital? There is no better place for ghost hunting excursions than a haunted hospital.

Some hauntings, however, are so mysterious that no one can explain them. Others are entirely baseless tales made up to scare people away from the hospital. Then there are the asylums, which are the most distressing of the lot. Before the availability of therapeutic pharmacological treatments, when mental illness was little understood, the only option to control anomalous conduct was by force. Rather than managing their illnesses at home with their families, the mentally ill were locked up by the thousands in giant institutions meant to function similarly to prisons.

The main distinction was that prison inmates were not subjected to the brutal and painful treatments as people with mental health conditions.

Large asylums were designed to resemble castles, with barred windows and multiple wings, each with its yards and buildings. The wards resembled prisons rather than hospitals - the only color in the drab institutional environment was the uniforms worn by staff and patients. Walls were often padded to prevent self-harm or suicide attempts. There was no belief that mental illness could be cured or managed, only that it could be contained, so minimal care was provided within asylums. Patients were tied into their beds for most of the day and left alone in tiny cells for long periods without proper nutrition or hygiene care; they were subjected to electroshock therapy and ice baths.

Checking into a crazy asylum was simple, but checking out was nearly impossible. So many patients lived and died there, only to reappear as spirits trapped in the structure that claimed their lives. It's one thing to see an apparition, but it's quite another to come across one who is mentally ill.

As my fascination with old hospitals from another age grew, I began compiling a list of some of the most intriguing, eerie, and disturbing abandoned hospitals and asylums worldwide. The abandoned hospitals on this list have histories that are dark and often violent. They've seen American wars, pandemics, terrible epidemics, and of course, death. These buildings represent a time when there were fewer safety nets for the sick and dying in society. They remind us of how much safer our world is today. So, what do you think? Would you dare explore these haunted asylums and hospitals on one of your next adventures?

Let's get started

1. Ararat Lunatic Asylum

Ararat Lunatic Asylum came into being on the banks of Lake Ararat, near the ancient Armenian village of Sis, in 1847. The asylum was established by Dr. C.W. Leadbeater and Professor Mieczyslaw Kozminski, aided by medical staff members at what was then called Liverpool Royal Infirmary. But despite its unique location and English name, Ararat was far from a luxury institution. Its main buildings were constructed from mud bricks, and it could house only thirty patients at a time in primary cells - cramped spaces where they were locked up alone for days or even weeks without stimulation or contact with other humans.

Ararat Lunatic Asylum was designed to give patients a chance to recover their mental health and help them lead normal lives once more. But it did not attempt to cure patients of their madness, and it failed entirely in its hope.

Medical treatment for the insane was revolutionized in England during the nineteenth century. The number of psychiatrists working in the country rose dramatically, by around 100 percent between 1843 and 1858, with a further 200% increase required by

1860. A variety of new treatments were introduced, from morphine to chloral hydrate. The medical profession believed that insanity could be cured, and many people with mental illness were released into society - often against their will - as they were deemed cured.

Ararat, on the other hand, did not operate in such utopian atmosphere. It was a grim place where the mentally ill were sent to survive as best they could simply. Members of its staff even criticized the asylum for its cruel conditions. In 1883, Dr. Edward Wilson wrote that 'the striking thing about Ararat is the utter absence of any attempt to supply any form of occupation for the patients'.

Newspaper reports from the time confirm this picture of Ararat as a cruel institution where patients were mistreated and neglected. One report from 1889 claimed that 'at Ararat asylum, the patients are starved and ill-treated'. Another stated that 'there is just as much neglect in our local asylums as there is in the prisons'.

The mistreatment of patients at Ararat was not limited to the lack of mental stimulation they received. There were also allegations, following an inquiry into conditions at the asylum, that staff members physically abused patients. One patient, Ellen Leighton, died after being hit on her head several times by a member of staff called Florence Baker; Baker claimed she was acting for the patient's good as she was 'a violent maniac'.

Ararat Lunatic Asylum was a morbidly grand place for those who ended up in its care, with the military-style buildings surrounded by a high fence and an impressive statue of St. Anne on a nearby hill. (The sculpture has since been removed). But the reality of life in Ararat was far from pleasant. Patients spent their days locked away alone in darkened rooms without stimulation or human contact, and many died as a result - some within months despite the best efforts of staff to cure them.

The first patients were admitted to Ararat Lunatic Asylum in 1847, and it soon became clear that it was not what Dr. Leadbeater had intended when he founded the institution.

To get to the asylum's main building, patients had to trudge through the shallows of the lake, wading through swampy marshlands that gave way to willow trees and reeds and patches of reeds. They also had to negotiate muddy paths cut by cows belonging to the village's inhabitants.

The lunatics were not fed in any meaningful sense and were fed on bread and water gruel, a traditional Armenian dish made from crushed wheat grains. The lunatic would have faced grim days alone in their cell with little or no stimulation, except perhaps for piano practice arranged for them by Kozminski himself.

On the other hand, there was plenty of stimulation for Kozminski and Leadbeater: the asylum's patients were kept totally on edge, forced to move in complete darkness, and kept chattering ceaselessly. They knew that they had been locked up in the asylum for a reason but were not told just why. Most of those treated at Ararat suffered from dementia, but there was some controversy about whether their afflictions resulted from physical or psychological causes. Leading lights in psychiatry such as Sigmund Freud sided with the psychological theory to explain them - but renowned psychiatrist Maudsley denied this was possible without physical causes. The actual cause of Ararat's patients' behavior remains unknown

The asylum was a strange place, but it was no stranger than the patient who ran it. Dr. C.W. Leadbeater's own career as a psychiatrist had been marred by controversy: he was dismissed from his job at the Royal Infirmary in Liverpool in 1892 for encouraging occultism among staff and patients alike. Unperturbed, Leadbeater left and created Ararat Lunatic Asylum with Kozminski, adopting a new name and even claiming to be part of a new race called the Aryans - the master race (according to Nazi ideology).

His theories were published in influential medical journals, some arguing that insanity was triggered by nutritional deficiencies rather than organic causes - an idea that still has currency today.

But as word of Ararat's peculiar treatments spread, the asylum was closed in 1851 after it had been open for only a year. It was little more than a footnote in psychiatric history, but Leadbeater's theories had been discredited by the end of the century and the cost of patients' care with it. Ararat eventually closed its doors forever.

The Ararat Lunatic Asylum was previously known as Aradale. Aradale and its two sister asylums in Kew and Beechworth were built to house the expanding number of 'lunatics' in Victoria's colony.

Construction began in 1860, and the facility opened to the public in 1865. In 1998, it was declared defunct as an asylum. Aradale housed up to 900 patients per year at its peak and is a vast complex with up to 70 ancient abandoned structures. Take a tour of the opulent wards and halls of the Victorian institution that has treated and housed the mentally ill for almost 140 years.

2. Beechworth Lunatic Asylum

The Beechworth Asylum opened for patient admission in October 1867, following campaigning by the Beechworth Municipal Council. Due to a lack of more appropriate housing, patients were previously confined to the town's jail.

When the first patients arrived, men worked as farm laborers, carpenters, blacksmiths, painters, shoemakers, and tailors, while women worked as launderers, knitters, sewists, and domestics.

Recreational activities were first introduced around 1880, according to archives. Additional structures were built in the years that followed to accommodate the need for patients to be housed in the area.

The Wangaratta Ladies Auxiliary was founded in 1938, and community members played an active role in contributing to the comfort and interests of patients. The Mental Health Authority adopted the "Open Door" policy in 1952, and the outer wall was demolished in 1955.

By the 1960s, the hospital had developed a Nurse Training School and an associated Nurses' Home, resulting in significant advancements in nursing education.

The departments of Mental Retardation and Mental Hospital were officially split in 1962.

Several wards were restored, renamed, and reopened as a Training Centre in 1964, with the sole purpose of caring for and training more than 200 people with intellectual disabilities.

The Mental Health Act of 1959 established the Psychiatric Hospital in 1977. There were fewer customers in the late 1980s and early 1990s due to the growth of other residential options (day placements, education, job, and recreational possibilities).

By 1992, all clients with intellectual disabilities had been discharged from the hospital and placed in alternative settings. The Psychiatric Hospital had 130 beds by 1993; however, only 20 were available for acute adult patients and more than 60 for geriatric patients.

By 1996, the hospital had expanded to include two psycho-geriatric wards (Emerald and Amethyst), the

Kerferd Acute Clinic, Willow, and external housing on Gilchrest Avenue and Mayday Court. Decommissioning began that year, and the property was designated to the National Register of Historic Places.

In February 2012, a three-week excavation of a previously unexcavated burial ground area in the grounds of Beechworth Lunatic Asylum uncovered the remains of an old cemetery — overcrowded and overgrown with flowers.

The discovery was made at a spot marked on plans for the site to become part of a new visitor center, which would include an exhibition about asylum life and exhibits for visitors to explore. The Sydney Morning Herald reports that forensic archaeologists revealed "an unknown number of burials" were found during the dig.

The Beechworth Lunatic Asylum operated from 1867 to 1995. The building, which operated as a mentally ill hospital, was closed in November 1995 and listed on the NSW State Heritage Register.

In 2007, the facility was developed into a partially functioning museum as part of the VELA (Villages to Experience Local Area) project. In 2011, information panels about the asylum were installed during renovations.

Archaeologist David Heslop said that approximately 30 burials were found during this excavation, but it is unknown how many more are still undiscovered throughout the asylum's complex grounds. During construction in 2005, a body was discovered buried beneath the sand in a riverbed on hospital land.

The dig occurred on land that is to become part of a new visitor center.

"These remains are likely the remains of people who had passed away while living and were buried in an asylum cemetery, although it's not known whether there was one cemetery or if there were multiple cemeteries," said Heslop.

"It's possible that due to population surges or the closure of other [asylum] sites, these people could have been transferred to Beechworth."

Beechworth Lunatic Asylum ghost story

The first Australian ghost story I learned was the Beechworth Lunatic Asylum, which served as a local mental institution and prison from 1838 to 1972 - long before its disappearance into a post-modern ruin.

It was at the Beechworth Lunatic Asylum that one day, just like now, patients were laid out in their dormitory beds when one of them got up from his bed and walked straight through the wall. The bemused hospital staff repeatedly tried to find out what made him do it but could only come up with two possible explanations: either an evil spirit had possessed him, or he had suffered a stroke.

The hospital's superintendent, Dr. John Withers, was less inclined to believe in ghosts and thought that perhaps he had had a stroke or suffered a brain aneurysm. The hospital staff never saw the patient again, but some say that you can still see him on moonless nights wandering the asylum grounds.

His name is believed to have been Ted Cooper - or possibly Ted Comber. There are innumerable ghost stories about Beechworth Lunatic Asylum. They are all told in hushed voices by those who grew up around it - and some even claim that if you go out onto the asylum's grounds on Halloween night, you can still hear a man screaming for mercy.

Beechworth Lunatic Asylum was the former site of a prison built in 1838 by John Thomas Nairn, who discovered gold in Victoria. When it was leased to the State of Victoria and became an asylum, it housed those who had received one year or more sentence for crimes such as arson, murder, burglary, and robbery. Beechworth Lunatic Asylum was also where many intellectuals and political activists were sent when they were incarcerated. Alongside the ax murderers and serial killers you would expect to find there, many political prisoners at Beechworth were sent there to express their dissatisfaction with their treatment by correctional officers or other inmates.

Perhaps it is the political prisoners who haunt Beechworth Lunatic Asylum. It is said that they still walk the asylum's corridors at night, banging on doors and walls and screaming for help.

Or perhaps it is the ghost of Dr. John Withers, former superintendent of the institution which died in 1897, who has been seen walking around his old institution late at night wearing a long black cloak and carrying a lantern. Some believe that this might not be his ghost but rather a prankster playing out a local legend.

Nearly all of Beechworth Lunatic Asylum ghost stories are embroidered with the legend that once you leave the asylum grounds, the gates will creak on their hinges and close behind you. Wandering into town, you can hear your footsteps echoing through dark passageways while the moans of former patients echo behind you. You can see shadows flitting in shadows, only to disappear when you turn your head.

But are they ghosts?

Sometimes people believe they have seen figures inside the asylum's walls - a man dressed in old-fashioned clothes, who has been seen walking down the corridors or climbing steps lit by moonlight. This could be explained by photographs taken on moonless nights.

3. Nummela Sanatorium

Nummela Sanatorium was constructed in the late 1800s. It was meant as a place where the municipal hospital patients were transferred to. The building housed tuberculosis patients from 1888 until it closed in 1984, and its building has since been torn down. The Sanatorium's nickname, "The House of Terror," is based on the stories of people who had negative experiences while they worked there, both nurses and doctors. In the early 1980s, students from Helsinki Polytechnic University made up ghost stories to frighten their classmates about what they had witnessed during fieldwork at Nummela Sanatorium. The stories, particularly those of the ghosts of two head nurses, have spread on the Internet, and Nummela Sanatorium has become a popular urban legend in Finland.

The original sanatorium building was designed by architect Gustaf Nyström and comprised two-floor levels. It is believed that there is a tunnel underneath the structure that connects to the hospital in Mäntsälä. This is because patients who could not cross Mäntsälä by foot were transported back and forth through this tunnel. In addition to the main building in Nummela, a smaller medical station was used to treat tuberculosis patients from other municipalities. There was also a small building in the complex for tuberculosis patients in the final stages of their disease. These patients would spend their final days at the Sanatorium and die shortly after they arrived. The small building, called "the Chapel," was isolated from the Sanatorium by a hedge.

Nummela Sanatorium remained in operation until 1984, when it had to close due to its deteriorating condition. Prior to its closure, the municipality sold off all of its furnishings and equipment, and some of them ended up in private homes; for example, a bed that once belonged to a patient is now owned by a family who lives nearby.

Nummela Sanatorium is believed to have some spirits resulting from patients who died in the building. At least two ghosts have been reported by those who worked at the Sanatorium. One of these is a head nurse called Noora, and the other is a doctor called Paavo who worked at Nummela as a young doctor between 1939 and 1942. According to one report, Noora (who was also purportedly the ghost of an SS officer) hung herself after she became pregnant by her colleague, professor Kustaa Franzén. Nurse Nora Clark may have inspired Noora's name in Kenneth Fearing's "**The Big Clock**." Another story suggests that Noora committed suicide after she was unable to save Paavo from committing suicide.

Staff members have reported another ghost at the Sanatorium. As a young doctor in 1939, Paavo may have converted an old outhouse into Paavo's room. He would do his research on tuberculosis and other diseases that he treated at Nummela Sanatorium. Soon after he moved into this room, Paavo died of tuberculosis. Still, his body was buried elsewhere on the grounds of Nummela Sanatorium as the family could not afford to have a funeral for him.

This abandoned hospital, now called "The Ghost Hospital," was originally built in 1929 as a tuberculosis sanatorium for isolation and treatment of tuberculosis patients. The story goes that when World War II came along, this hospital was used as a Nazi military hospital, during which time it saw many wounded soldiers. This may be true; however, no documents have been found to prove this so far. Both Polish and Soviet troops occupied the hospital after World War II. The hospital was abandoned by the end of the sixties. It remained abandoned for several years until the Olesno Council eventually purchased it in 1980. The hospital now serves as a nursing home and funeral home under the name "Olesno Dom Tekniczny" which means "Olesno Home for Technicians."

The hospital has been known to many to be haunted, but there are no documented stories detailing haunting incidents. However, several reported phenomena and legends have been told about this building being haunted.

Several patients who died there, or who died shortly before their deaths, have been seen by residents of the nursing home and appeared as if they were walking the halls and corridors of the building. The apparitions are usually in regular clothing, such as normal everyday clothing. These reports may be false as people have mistaken the apparitions for another more famous hospital in Olesno called

"Olesno Dom Zabaw," which means "Olesno Children's Home." The latter hospital also has a long history of hauntings, which included many patients being restrained to beds. Also, there had been evidence of crossed radio waves found on recording devices placed within the facility on several occasions.

One of the most famous reports of paranormal activity is a story told to me by one of my classmates who had visited the hospital many years ago with a group of friends. This group made their way through the building, looking for answers and possibly ghostly evidence. They could locate an abandoned operating room that looked as though it were in great condition, completely untouched by time. Documents were stored inside, and old tools had remained intact as if they were still in use today. This area was not original to the building; it was added later in its history. It has been said that this room was used for Nazi medical experiments on human subjects. My classmate all but confirms this story. His group made their way out of the operating room and into the hallway. As they approached the end of the hall, they were met by a tall, thin man dressed in a white doctor's jacket. He was standing in front of a large window and just turned to look at them as if he knew they were coming and didn't care that they had entered his domain. The figure then vanished through the wall.

There have been many stories told regarding the patients that stay in this particular building. Many reports they have seen patients as young as five and over 100 years old. It has been said that the ghost of a girl has been seen near the front entrance, while a woman with long hair and a large hat has been seen in the old Chapel. Another woman was reportedly heard whispering, "Let me go."

On the same day, Paranormal Book Publishing will release an awesome haunting book titled "Ghosts of Olesno". This book will give more information about this haunted hospital along with many other local legends from this amazing town.

This hospital was listed as one of the topmost haunted places in Poland by Haunted Locations. This is a very detailed list and is worth browsing. It goes over many locations in Poland, and they are all worth checking out if you love to read about paranormal activity.

This hospital has also been placed on several other top 10 lists, such as the list of Top 10 Most Haunted Places in Europe. Even a recent study by European Hauntings Forum placed this hospital in its Top 20 most haunted locations in Central Europe. This amazing study covered many countries, including Austria, Bosnia & Herzegovina, Czech Republic, Estonia, Finland, Germany, Hungary, Latvia, Lithuania, Montenegro, and Poland.

The building sits on an awesome piece of land that is both secluded and beautiful. The building seems very strictly unoccupied as there appear to be no lights on or anything else that would indicate signs of life.

A small stone bridge next to the hospital crosses over a small creek leading into the Vistula river. This creek is part of a system of canals built in the late nineteenth century throughout Poland, and this was probably used as a water supply for the facility. The bridge itself is far from safe to cross, especially at night, as it has a slight tilt to one side, making it very rickety and hard to navigate. However, I am not aware of anyone who has been injured crossing over the bridge or around the hill.

The hospital itself is not hard to locate even in complete darkness as there are streetlights along the road leading up to it. The building is long and has some beautiful arched doorways with green roofing. The ground floor is basically a modern-looking hospital of which I can find no information. However, the upper floors have been abandoned for many years.

The building has a quaint chapel situated on the rooftop and two dormitories attached to one side of the main building. A lot of light and noise can be heard from below, indicating there must be people down below. Also, many tall windows seem to stare out into the darkness of the night sky, looking as though they could be watching you at any moment.

The Chapel itself has been reported as being haunted by multiple ghosts. It has been said that the ghost of a nun haunts this room and several floating orbs of light that appear out of nowhere and disappear into the walls. Many reports have been of an older man wearing a black coat or suit and hat, sitting on one of the pews and disappearing seconds later.

There are many different stories about who used to stay in this facility; however, there is no definitive answer. It is known that during its hay days, soldiers were treated here for injuries sustained in World War I and II.

Apparently, Nazi Germany took over running this hospital during WWII when Nazi Germany's forces occupied Poland. The Nazis used this facility for medical experiments and to test the effects of various drugs on humans. In this building alone, it is estimated that over 200,000 people died during the war.

Many different patients were housed here, from wounded soldiers to civilians and even Jews that were taken off trains arriving at the nearby train station. There have been multiple reports of screams coming from the chapel area at night and reports of seeing shadows moving around in the windows.

Some visitors have reported hearing crying babies at night, while others report seeing spirits roaming in the halls and rooms throughout this building. There have also been reports of a presence behind them when they visit, then suddenly being showered with glass fragments and wood from an unknown source.

4. Old Changi Hospital

The Old Changi Hospital has long been whispered as one of Singapore's most haunted places. Allegedly, many lives have ended in the hospital's hallways, and you've got to admit that it sounds like the perfect setting for a horror film. With all these spooky stories surrounding this place, I wonder what some of them are. And what about all those people who saw apparitions there? I'm sorry to say that your search ends here for any skeptics out there looking for evidence to debunk these stories.

First of all, I think it's important to know a little about the history of the Old Changi Hospital. It was built in 1935 and was originally called the Civil Hospital. In the Japanese Occupation, the hospital used to be a Prisoner-of-War (POW) camp for captured British soldiers. After World War II ended, it became a base for the British army until they left Singapore entirely in 1971. After that, the hospital became mainly used as an outpatient clinic and became part of the National University Hospital in 1981.

This is also where most of the alleged "sightings" took place.. Over the years; there were reports of floating objects and unexplained sounds in the hallways. Some people even claimed to have seen an old lady dressed in a long white gown walking down the corridors. And then there are those recurring stories about "the old man" who supposedly died of a heart attack while lying on a hospital bed and other apparitions. There's also an old tale about three nurses going crazy as they walked down the corridors one night, and when they came back, they quarreled with each other over something that didn't seem to be important.

I've visited this place myself but what I saw was nothing like what had been described in all those ghost stories. I went there to find out if there is any truth to the stories, and all I found was evidence of neglect. The Old Changi Hospital is a bit run down now, but it's still used as a medical facility. Surprisingly, there are no creepy present-day ghost stories to be found here, as far as I know. But if you still want to experience some spooky supernatural activity, then perhaps you ought to go visit the old Changi Hospital sometime soon... and bring along a pair of arm Wrestling Gloves for added protection.

Moving on from the old haunted hospital, it seems that the "Old Changi Cemetery" site is also haunted. It was turned into a park located in Pasir Ris today. Many people have claimed that paranormal activity has occurred here, some even saying that it is the source of the haunting of the old hospital. These ghost stories are things I haven't yet heard about from my friends, so I guess I'll just have to look into this some more...

It sounds like it might be an interesting place to visit someday. Maybe that's something worth checking out too sometime..

OCH is known for hiring spirit guides to help them pursue their work and keep an eye on things, which is why they are sometimes referred to as the "ghost hospital" There was also an incident in 1977 when a nurse apparently had a ghostly encounter with a bedridden patient there. It turns out that she had been "chosen" by the spirit. Reports of sighting and other supernatural activity at the OCH have been going on for years.

Since many famous people have had their surgeries here, some people say that these events may have made them famous. H. P. Yee, a lawyer and member of parliament, once said a ghostly encounter with an older man in OCH when he was brought in for an operation. He also said that the spirits visited him after it was done before leaving. However, this has been disputed. The site of the former OCH has long been part of Changi Village Park and is currently occupied by several structures. It's generally quiet there except for the odd passing jogger and some kites flying in the wind..

The bottom line is; some paranormal activity haunts old Changi Hospital... so be careful when you visit there.

5. Gonjiam Psychiatric Hospital

The abandoned Gonjiam Psychiatric Hospital is well-known in Korea and worldwide for its terrifying stories. Keep in mind that the structure isn't haunted by the spirits of ordinary people but by the deranged... CNN named it one of the strangest locales on the planet, confirming its notoriety.

Despite popular belief that the mental institution was shuttered in the 1990s due to violent patients and insane doctors, the truth is less spectacular. In actuality, it occurred as a result of economic downturns, which resulted in filthy conditions and sewage issues. The owner elected just to flee, and the fate of the patients remains unknown.

Even if there aren't any ghosts, the place is creepy with its rusted-out machinery and other hospital relics, filthy mattresses, and rubbish is strewn about. And, if it is haunted, it is simply curious visitors who continue to visit the abandoned asylum.

They aren't deterred by the fact that it is closed to the public and has unclean conditions. Locals are unwilling to give guidance to wandering adventurers, although this is also ineffective. The challenge of locating the location on your own, on the other hand, adds to the enjoyment of the journey. The hospital is situated on the outskirts of Gwangju, a small city in South Korea.

The history

Imagine walking through a hospital, only to find that it's completely abandoned. No nurses, no doctors...no patients. That's right — the doors are locked. Windows are broken and boarded up. And yet, something is screaming inside. What you've just seen is an almost perfect depiction of the Gonjiam Psychiatric Hospital in South Korea.

The hospital was shut down in June of 2018 for safety concerns and has since become one of the country's most popular ghost sites for people who want to be terrified with a group of friends while getting their adrenaline pumping from some good scares.

The Gonjiam Psychiatric Hospital was built in 1968 and opened its doors the following year. It was created as a national center for treatment for people living with mental disabilities. Now, it's widely accepted that it was never meant to be a place of healing or rehabilitation. (Of course, if you look at the conditions inside, you can see why.)

At the time of its construction, there were no severe laws on neuropsychiatric treatment in Korea (there are now). In other words, no way to prevent patients from being treated and abused. The hospital was closed in June of 2018 because of concerns for public safety. The public outcry was immediate and severe, but the government had little choice but to shut it down.

The hospital occupants were routinely subjected to physical abuse by their nurses, doctors, and other staff members. Slapping, choking, beating, burning: you name it, they did it.

One patient said that he "became so frightened that he would often pray to God for help and cry for someone to put an end to the terror." He died soon after of a complication from his injuries.

You need to see these photos to understand just how bad patients were treated. We're talking about people with mental illnesses who cannot respond appropriately to the terror they were experiencing. This doesn't matter, though: the abuse continued until they were released or died...which was often.

The hospital also performed unnecessary surgeries on its patients when it wasn't hurting them as a form of punishment. It's estimated that around 2,000 people died in this place while it was operating between 1968 and 2018.

At least 8,000 people died at this hospital before its closure in 2018.

The hospital was closed for various reasons, including some that have been confirmed by patients and staff who witnessed the horrors inside. Like the fact that it's located on top of an old burial ground, which is never a good sign for a place filled with people who are trying to heal their minds:

"[My friend] had stayed over at other dorms and experienced strange things but never like in this dorm. The entire dorm had the same problem. Noises, footsteps, this would happen when I was in my room alone, so I would ask my friend to sleep in my room so we could talk throughout the night. But as soon as my friend would get into the room and try to talk to me, all the noises that were being made in the other rooms would suddenly stop...like someone was telling them to stop making noise. It wasn't like it was just us who heard these noises. Other neighbors in our dorm had heard these things too."

Another reason was that patients were simply trying to escape this hellhole. In one instance, a patient escaped from his cell and killed a nurse (after which he was beaten by other staff members and later died). After this incident, patients were locked up more often than not, even if they weren't being punished for something they did wrong. (The doors didn't even have locks until 2005. In other words, they were useless.)

As a result, the hospital became a site for torture and abuse. And the way that patients were treated became more and more severe.

It didn't help that the hospital constantly lost power. Its generators kept going out (and they did not have enough). They had such a hard time getting them fixed that they started looking into building their own generator system "because there were so many complaints from patients about losing power."

Sometimes this caused them to lose power for just a few hours. Other times...it was for an entire day or two. And not to mention, there was "little to no maintenance on the buildings."

There were also incidents of fires at the hospital. "Patients had been set on fire by their wardens while they slept...When a patient was burnt so badly that they died, the wardens didn't even attempt to save them."

To be fair, though, there were times when patients escaped from the asylum. They were forced back inside because of bad weather, low morale, or needed medical treatment. And other times, family members would lock them in there for their safety.

Even though it's 2018, and we know that people living in South Korea are trying to heal their minds (and bodies), this is still happening. The reason is simple: they don't have enough medical professionals to take care of the growing number of people with mental illnesses (they don't even have enough facilities to house them).

It's estimated that there are over 1,400,000 living in South Korea today. Only about 84,000 of them are being treated for their conditions. That's only about 7%.

According to one account, a patient was locked in a solitary cell with no heat — and had no blankets — for nearly three weeks. Another patient was left naked outside in the cold night air because there were no more clothes for him to wear. The government is still paying the families of those who died to remove their bodies from the hospital. They had until September of 2018 to do so.

It's easy to see why people would feel moved by these stories — not just because the story itself is heartbreaking but also because it's a testament to the persistence of human nature. Stories like this aren't JUST about some forgotten place in South Korea, they're about a period in time that illustrates how society can be cruel and careless with its health and lives.

At least in the past, Korea never boasted one of those high-tech hospitals that give you every conceivable treatment imaginable while ensuring that you're mentally healthy and safe. On the contrary, the hospital was nothing more than some cold, dark rooms and cement floors. There were no comfortable chairs or soft blankets — just many rusty tools that no one used very often.

But thanks to the government's decision to shut it down and clean up, they are now turning the place into a cultural heritage site. It will open its doors soon in 2019 as an open-air museum for people who want to really feel what it was like inside the hospital.

The hospital has been demolished and is now a park for visitors to explore the abandoned building or take in an exhibition to get some context about how mental health care has developed over time in South Korea.

The hospital is being turned into a park that will be turned into an open-air museum.

Though it's been closed for nearly a year, there are still reports of people getting hurt or even dying while attempting to visit the site. There have also been reports of trespassers moving things around and breaking windows to create an even scarier atmosphere.

Unfortunately, it's already too late for Gonjiam Psychiatric Hospital. But at least the government is doing something to restore it to its original purpose

But enough about why this hospital was closed. Let's talk about the reason why it became a popular place for teenagers to visit: its insanity coupled with the ghost stories they've heard about this place.

So, it's long been an urban legend that this hospital is haunted. Some of the stories are true, like how some of the former patients died there and never left. This has led to overcrowding and odd paranormal activity.

These stories have circulated for a long time now, but their popularity only grew once the hospital was shut down. At its peak, over 3,000 teenagers were visiting this place each year (including at least three who died from falling down the spiral staircase).If you've ever heard of that movie The Ring, they used this place as inspiration for it (it was filmed in Japan, though).

The hospital has also appeared in other movies such as A Tale of Two Sisters (2003), White: The Melody of the Curse (2007), and Witch's Romance (2014).

There's no denying that this place is beautiful, but it's also a little bit creepy.

There were even reports of people using its architecture as a photo opportunity to make this place look cooler. And while it looks like an awesome anime set, it's not safe for people to go inside the building since parts of it are on the verge of collapse.

Some studies have actually been done on this abandoned hospital in South Korea. One study was done in 2012 to see if there were any traces left behind from when the hospital operated during its heyday.

Another study found that the air quality inside the building was still relatively good in 2014. That's a big deal since it was estimated that there was five years' worth of dust inside this place. It's hard to imagine if it's a place that no one cared about for nearly two decades until someone decided to save it.

Some people have been trying to save this place since at least 2005 when the hospital stopped admitting new patients (but they couldn't find anyone who would buy it from them). So they closed its doors and locked them up tight so people wouldn't get inside and hurt themselves (or get hurt by the other people who had already been there too long.)

But some people did still break-in.

6. Waverly Hills Sanatorium, Louisville, Ky

The Waverly Hills Sanatorium was a former tuberculosis hospital in Louisville that was shut down in 1996 due to the widespread use of antibiotics. Now it has been repurposed and is now open as an art and history museum. In addition to this hospital being closed down for good, Waverly Hills also had several other unusual features, including catacombs with nearly 3 million skeletons dating back to the 19th century and an underground cavern with over 100 human remains that have not yet been identified.

Originally Waverly Hills was a farmhouse built in 1883 for wealthy businessman Nathan S. Davis. After Davis died in 1892, his widow and daughters converted the home into a TB sanatorium. In 1910, the Sanatorium was sold to the state of Kentucky with the understanding that it would be used for people afflicted with tuberculosis. After several expansions and renovations, Waverly Hills opened as a hospital on October 1, 1916.

Waverly Hills Sanatorium had about 560 patient beds in its peak years and held more than 25,000 patients during its operation from 1910 until 1962, when it closed its doors permanently. The medical treatment at the Sanatorium had many unique features. One of them is an underground morgue for storing coldstorage cadavers until they could be autopsied. This crematory could capture up to 350 pounds of bones and ashes per cycle, underground catacombs with almost 3 million human skeletons, and an underground cavern with over 100 bodies that have not been identified.

The first floor of Waverly Hills Sanatorium contained an admission area and areas to treat tuberculosis patients, such as the open-air solarium. In 1915, Waverly Hills was expanded to include a Children's Building where children and their families could be treated for TB from all across the world. In 1916, an open-air TB pavilion was added, capable of treating 880 patients at any given time. There were also several private rooms for patients who could afford to pay for their own treatment. In the 1940s and 50s, Waverly Hills became a popular place for tuberculosis patients in the United States and many from abroad to receive treatment due to its popularity in treating wealthy citizens at the time.

Waverly Hills gained much media attention due to its unique architecture and architectural style constructed during that period. Many medical journals and newspapers in the United States and abroad wrote articles about the architectural style and its unusual art installation displays. In addition to Waverly Hills being a hospital, it also contained a variety of other unique features that were added over time such as a radio station that was used to receive reports from around the world, an underground cavern that held 100 unidentified bodies, and a morgue for storing cold storage bodies until they could be autopsied.

In 1973, containment walls were constructed around Waverly Hills to help contain any molds or bacteria inside the unique structure. The basement level was also sealed off at this time to protect patients who lived there from any possible disease. On March 31, 1993, Waverly Hills Sanatorium officially closed down. After the hospital had closed down in 1996, it was abandoned and was left unused for nearly 20 years.

In February of 2013, Eric Holter bought Waverly Hills for 1 dollar, intending to convert it into a non-tourist art and history museum known as the House of Tomorrow. However, before Holter could renovate Waverly Hills, he had to deal with an underground cavern holding human remains from the many TB patients that had died at the hospital during its operation from 1910 until 1962. $100,000 was spent to seal off the chamber and the bodies inside of it, and for a few years, afterward, the chamber was used as part of Waverly Hills' art exhibits.

Today, Waverly Hills is a fully-renovated building that has been converted into a museum with over 1 million square feet of retail space and over 100 art galleries. The museum includes many different exhibits and displays, including underground chambers, catacombs, and rooms with human remains. Another unique feature featured at the House of Tomorrow is an interactive exhibit called "The Unidentified" that lets visitors touch DNA samples taken from unidentified dead people to see which samples belong to who.

The haunted history

The abandoned Waverly Hills Sanatorium in Louisville, Kentucky, previously housed a large number of tortured souls. This was a facility designed to house tuberculosis patients in the hopes of discovering a cure and allowing them to return to their lives and loved ones.

Unfortunately, this was not the case for many who passed through its doors, and some of their souls now linger within its confines.

One of the most technologically advanced tuberculosis hospitals in the world at the time. Major Thomas H. Hays purchased the site for Waverly Hills Sanatorium in 1883. He needed a place for his daughters to go to school. On the site, he built a one-room schoolhouse and employed Lizzie Lee Hawkins as a teacher. She called the school "Waverley Hill" after Sir Walter Scott's "Waverley Novels." The Waverly Hills Sanatorium got its name from here.

Tuberculosis disease, also known as the "White Plague," was on the rise in Kentucky. The creation of the Waverly Hills Sanatorium, which began in 1908, was spurred by this. The Tuberculosis Board purchased the land on which the hospital was built, which was originally a two-story structure meant to house 40-50 tuberculosis patients safely.

All of the Tuberculosis patients from the city hospital were moved to temporary tents on the grounds of Waverly Hills on August 31, 1912, because the city hospital was overburdened with TB cases and unable to handle the surge of patients.

For advanced cases, the facility was expanding to accommodate another 40 patients. A children's pavilion with 50 beds was erected in 1914. The hospital's capacity was raised to 130 patients as a result of this. The children's ward was established to shelter tuberculosis-affected children and youngsters whose parents had the disease. The hospital was fully staffed when it opened on July 26, 1910.

Patients, doctors, and nurses became residents and lived within the Sanatorium after they entered the facility. This was a self-sufficient neighborhood with its zip code. They established their radio station and cultivated their food.

Sanatoriums were built on high hills surrounded by woodlands at the time to provide quiet and tranquility. Fresh air, excellent diet, and sunshine, together with professional medical supervision, were thought to aid in the cure of the disease. The staff did everything they could to maintain a positive atmosphere and keep the patients happy. This was also considered to keep patients alive longer and prevent them from succumbing to the sickness.

The doctors' operations on patients were as dreadful as the sickness itself. Many of the patients died as a result of the experimental medical procedures. Lobectomy and Pneumectomy were two therapies that included doctors surgically removing infected sections of the lung and the entire lung in some cases.

Thoracoplasty, or removing numerous rib bones from the chest wall to collapse a lung, was another operation. During this time, it was usual for patients to require the removal of 7-8 ribs on average.

The "Sun-treatment" also proposed that if a patient bathed in the sun, the bacteria that caused tuberculosis would be killed. The doctors would also implant a balloon into the patients' lungs and fill it with air to aid breathing. Unfortunately, these treatments were ineffectual and did not result in a true cure.

The staff attempted to boost patient morale by allowing family members to visit. There was a visiting day where family members of patients may come into the institution and visit their sick loved ones, unaware that this was an airborne sickness at the time.

Sadly, many of the patients did not survive their stay at Waverly Hills. The death rate was around one per day, and as the sickness spread, this figure climbed dramatically. A special chute named "The Body Chute" was erected to allow the dead to be taken out at night, preventing patients from seeing the bodies of deceased patients. The bodies would be carried onto the train and taken away from the Sanatorium, which was right behind it, where the chute stopped.

According to one of the many hauntings recorded at Waverly Hills Sanitorium, a little child named Timmy has been seen with a leather ball and is assumed to have fallen off from the roof where the kids used to play. There was an investigation into whether Timmy was pushed or fell over the top, but no conclusion was reached.

Room 502, where the head nurse stays, is another story.

She was discovered dead in her room in 1928, apparently hanging herself from an exposed pipe or light fixture. She was 29 years old, unmarried, and pregnant. She allegedly committed suicide because she was depressed about the circumstances. Another nurse, who was subsequently found in Room 502, is likely to have jumped to her death from the top-level, though it's also possible she was pushed. There is no evidence report to support either of these claims. These are just some of the few of the hospital's documented hauntings.

After the discovery of the antibiotic Streptomycin, which cured tuberculosis, the hospital was closed in 1961. The hospital was gradually vacated once the patients were given this treatment. After the Sanatorium closed, it was quarantined and reopened as the Woodhaven Geriatric Center, a geriatric facility for individuals with dementia and mobility issues, closed in 1981. The hospital is still closed today.

7. Hospital For Mental Illness In Whittingham

In Lancaster, England, three mental asylums were declared entirely full in the late nineteenth century, driving the region to create Whittingham Mental Hospital, which opened its doors in 1873. At a time when widespread institutionalization was thought to be the best way to treat the mentally ill, the hospital was held in high regard in the community. Whittingham owned a church, several farms, a railway, a telephone exchange, a post office, reservoirs, and a brewery. Not to mention the symphony, brass band, ballroom, and butcher.

It began with a capacity of 1100 patients, but various annexes, including a sanatorium for people with infectious disorders, were quickly erected. Whittingham became the largest mental hospital in the United Kingdom, with a total capacity of 3,533 patients.

You may be wondering where all these "lunatics" came from. The short explanation is that most of the patients were not certifiably insane, to begin with. Extreme poverty appears to have a way of causing people to behave out in ways that aren't deemed normal. Whittingham was expressly developed for these "pauper lunatics."

It was converted into an asylum where the government admitted people who had no one to pay for their treatment. Historians have been doubtful of how deranged these destitute lunatics truly were. Most intake records were painfully unclear, with no annotations other than "crazy seaman" or "severe insanity." According to the records, these patients spent the rest of their lives at Whittingham.

Despite such a low incidence of patient recovery, Whittingham was regarded as a pioneer in electroencephalograms (EEGs), having experimented with the treatment on patients no less. For some, the technology was an excellent rehabilitation tool; for others, it was the polar opposite.

Twentieth-century England was a combustible country, and Whittingham witnessed some of history's darkest atrocities. Many of the hospital's doctors were drafted during World War I, while the nurses volunteered. The largest mental institution in the United Kingdom became severely understaffed.

Nonetheless, in 1918, the hospital's New West Annexe was adapted to treat war casualties for one grueling year. People who died there were laid to rest in a private cemetery. During World War II, from 1939 through 1946, two further wards were repurposed to treat both military and civilian victims.

After the great wars, one would assume that the load on Whittingham's patient care would ease. Sadly, the worst was yet to come.

Some employees observed significant cruelty and ill-treatment of patients and fraud in hospital management in the 1960s. The Student Nurses Association filed a complaint in 1967, but it did not go far. Whittingham's head male nurse collected the pupils, threatened them with libel and slander, and warned them to "put up or shut up."

The students were kept silent for a time, but after more individuals witnessed the brutality, the Hospital Management Committee was forced to investigate. What they uncovered regarding Whittingham's patient care was upsetting.

Patients in Ward 3, a male ward, were exposed to a "wet towel treatment." Nurses would put a damp towel or sheet around the patient's neck till they calmed down and fell unconscious for patients who couldn't behave themselves. Two additional nurses on Ward S2 would pour methylated spirits into the slippers and pockets of patients' bathrobes and light them on fire as a brutal punishment. Ward 16's ladies received the worst treatment of all.

To deter poor conduct, patients were often confined outside in all weather or washrooms and cupboards. Ailments of patients were not treated, and they were sometimes merely fed bread and jam, which was served as slops. Some nurses imposed hydration restrictions before and after meals, while others shackled rebellious patients to their beds while wearing only vests. The hair of one woman dragged her around. Surprisingly, this terrible ward had been supervised by the identical Catholic sister for 47 years.

Whittingham Hospital appeared to have devolved into anarchy during its long years of operation. Cockroaches, ants, and even mice plagued the wards, creeping over patients who could not leave their beds.

The majority of the facility was at dangerously low temperatures—46 degrees Fahrenheit or less. Between wards, the hospital workers fostered a culture of petty thievery. Serious fraud and embezzlement in the higher echelons ripped money right out of patients' pockets. Instead of building luxury condos for hospital administrators, money allocated for patient care was diverted.

When the crimes at Whittingham were revealed, the head nurse and head matron retired early. Two additional nurses were found guilty of theft, and another was sentenced to prison for manslaughter when an elderly patient he abused died.

All we know for certain about Whittingham's patient mistreatment is what student nurses and patients could prove in court. But everyone knew that wasn't even close to the entire magnitude of suffering at Whittingham throughout the years.

Following the investigation, the hospital limped on under the watchful eyes of administrators, bearing a dark name and numerous accounts of abuse. Despite efforts to transform the hospital into something new, frightening remnants from its eerie past remained to tell the story that the patients couldn't.

Lawrence Butterfield worked at Whittingham Facility in the mid-1980s and recalled strange events at the hospital after its darkest days were passed. Working the night shift, Butterfield was primed to be startled by things that go bump in the night.

But nothing seemed to bother him until one night when all the patients had gone to bed when he talked with another staff nurse. As she watched Butterfield, his coworker grew extremely quiet, and her face distorted into an expression of uncertainty and terror. When he questioned what was wrong, she replied she had seen a monkey figure hovering just above his shoulder. It has vanished before Bufferfield could notice, but both nurses were shaken.

Whittingham's entire staff had an aversion to one particular corridor of the hospital. It was "notorious...for strange occurrences," according to Butterfield. This one corridor was filled with windows that peered onto older wards crammed with decrepit beds and furnishings from Whittingham's dark past, unexplainable sounds, and unexpected power outages, to name a few of the bizarre events personnel and patients had. However, because it acted as a shortcut through the hospital, they used it frequently. Butterfield had got the unsettling impression that someone was watching him in the corridor, scaring him enough to flee.

Whittingham Hospital closed in 1995 due to a poor reputation, declining patient load, and an increasingly unpleasant atmosphere. As one might anticipate, the abandoned hospital has gained a new reputation for strange occurrences. Voices can be heard behind locked doors, and weird sights have sent several nighttime thrill-seekers hurrying to exit the premises.

With its history of locking up the poor, experimenting with treatments, enduring the pressures of two wars, and the rampant patient mistreatment that ensued, the hospital appeared to indulge in all the worst aspects of mass institutionalization. It's no surprise that the hospital's numerous wards send shivers down any visitor's spine.

Some may argue that the tormented patients of Whittingham never obtained true justice for the staff's actions, and they may seek vengeance on whoever remains in the buildings. But, save from the occasional trespasser, Whittingham's life and suffering are over, and the buildings continue to deteriorate.

8. Lunatic Asylum In Trans-Allegheny

In 1858, the municipality of Weston, West Virginia, began construction on an insane asylum. The project, driven by jail labor, was an unparalleled enterprise that took a long time to complete—construction was halted during the Civil War and began in 1862. The hospital was established on 666 acres of land since it was widely known that pollution from cities was a major cause of insanity. The most sophisticated treatment for the mentally sick would be fresh air and wide places.

The Trans-Allegheny Lunatic Asylum aimed for self-sufficiency, with a farm, dairy, waterworks, and cemetery. The hospital, the world's second-biggest hand-cut stone building (the Kremlin was greater), formally opened its doors in 1864. In 1873, a separate portion for African Americans was built out of need.

Despite its enormous grounds, Trans-Allegheny was only intended to hold 250 people. But it quickly changed. By 1880, there were 717 patients; by 1938, there were 1,661 patients; by 1949, there were more than 1,800 patients; and the patient population peaked at 2,400 in 1950.

The institution housed "epileptics, alcoholics, drug addicts, and non-educable mental defectives," according to a 1938 study by medical organizations. Perhaps they failed to mention, or perhaps it was later, that the hospital also housed children with Down syndrome and diabetes, disabled veterans with nowhere else to go, patients with syphilis before penicillin was available, and one couple with AIDS who had their apartment.

As it turns out, the hospital's nicest therapies were probably fresh air and distance from the rush and bustle of the cities. Frontal lobotomies and electroshock therapy were frequently used to help the most difficult patients calm down or put enough terror in them that they would obey.

Overcrowding began to take its toll on the university, as it did on many other large institutions at the period, fairly early on. In 1949, the Charleston Gazette published a series of exposés on the hospital, noting terrible hygiene as well as a lack of supplies, furniture, lighting, and heating.

Despite a relative drop inpatient population, matters worsened throughout the 1970s and 1980s. Reports of patients murdering other patients went uninvestigated, and female nurses and personnel were frequently abused. One nurse went missing, only to be discovered dead nearly two months later at the bottom of an empty stairway. Following that, doctors and personnel began pulling out all the stops—patients who could not be controlled were now confined in cages.

It's safe to say that no one will ever know the entire scope of patient mistreatment at Trans-Allegheny. The hospital's records are incredibly incomplete—many people who checked in never seemed to check out. Headstones are missing from the hospital's private cemetery. Others are simply numbered bricks with no information about their occupants.

Hundreds of people are known to have perished in the hospital. However, some believe there could have been thousands due to poor record-keeping. According to Andrea Lamb, a tour guide at the now-defunct facility, families were sometimes prevented from contacting their loved ones who were committed to the hospital. "They were advised that if they ever received a letter from them, they should never open it."

Years of press coverage have detailed Weston residents' complaints about hearing patient screams outside the 666-acre campus. In the late 1980s, city officials determined it was time to establish a new mental facility and began plans to convert Trans-Allegheny into a tiny prison.

In the end, the hospital closed in 1994 due to concerns over patient care, never to reopen. Unfortunately, many of the patients who had spent most of their lives at Trans-Allegheny were transferred to other facilities, only to relapse into mental illness or die inexplicably shortly afterward.

Despite being designated a National Historic Landmark while still in service, plans to reuse the structure into a Civil War Museum were thwarted due to fire code violations. For ten years, the mental asylum stood mostly empty until the state auctioned it off to Joe Jordan, a private entrepreneur, in 2007.

After millions of dollars in restorations and asbestos removal, Jordan and his family repurposed the building for concerts, festivals, and haunted hospital tours. Today, they provide paranormal tours six days a week, which have become increasingly popular since the building was featured on multiple ghost hunting shows.

While many owners of old buildings that have been repurposed as haunted houses must make some effort to market the structure's concept, Trans-dark Allegheny's history does it all by itself. The building manager, Rebecca Jordan Gleason, stated, "I don't want to believe in ghosts or the supernatural, but I've seen things here that are difficult to explain in any other way."

Most visitors never fail to notice some weird incident that they can't explain—battery loss, chilly areas, voices, bizarre figures on heat-seeking cameras, and so on. Many people claim to have heard gurneys being wheeled along lengthy corridors and screams coming from the electroshock area. Others claim to have seen full-body apparitions of patients.

Some of the ghosts who remain in the hospital appear to be in good spirits, chuckling and laughing throughout the facility. Others issue plain and scary cautions to flee. Visitors to the hospital may become ill after leaving, experiencing tremors, or feeling light-headed.

The bulk of ghost sightings at Trans-Allegheny appear to be one-of-a-kind, which is not surprising given the large number of people who lived, suffered, and died at the hospital. There is, however, one boy in particular who is repeatedly spotted standing unmoving in one room's corner.

Grant Wilson of The Atlantic Paranormal Society claimed to have seen this youngster but received a better display than others. He claimed the phantom put his hands over its head and appeared to be "sucked out of the room." Another ghost, commonly known as Jacob, resembles a soldier and frequently walks around the Civil War wing.

While strange occurrences happen everywhere over the ancient hospital, everyone agrees that the fourth level is the most haunted. On the usually empty floor, strange sounds, hammering, voices, and hushed discussions can be heard. The ghosts up there enjoy keeping people on their toes. Gleason reportedly saw 40 open doors on the fourth-floor corridor smash at the same time. "One would be fairly frightening," Gleason added. "Forty at the same time was terrifying."

9. Lier Sykehus Psychiatric Hospital

Lier Sykehus is a psychiatric hospital located in the Lier municipality in Buskerud, Norway. Originally, it was known as the Lier Asylum and the Lier Psychiatric Hospital. The hospital first opened its doors in 1926 with twelve patients. Four of the buildings were demolished in 1985, leaving just building numbers H, C, and G. Victor Nordan was the structure's architect.

About a half-hour from Oslo, this asylum was opened in 1926 and today is considered one of the most haunted hot spots in the country. Between 1945 and 1974, the hospital was notorious for conducting experiments on its patients involving the use of all sorts of bizarre drugs. After its closure, the hospital became a nursing home until it closed down in 1986.

This hospital has a chilling reputation for being haunted. Patients have reported seeing nurses holding others underwater in the hospital's pool, hearing voices from the walls and ceilings, and seeing doors opening independently. The hospital has even been home to several violent murders in the past. Patients have claimed to see doors opening and closing by themselves, screams coming from the walls and ceilings (even when no one else is around), and elevator doors opening to give way to empty floors. Some of the hospital's patients were so violent that they had been kept in padded rooms with locked doors, and even in those conditions, when staff members would enter the room to tend to them, they would find blood smeared on the walls. Rumor has it that one patient was given electroshock therapy every day for several years until he died of a heart attack at age 31 because he allegedly showed no response to any other treatment.

Most people believed that ghosts and spirits are wandering around. Some say this causes strange noises in the night – a sound like something moving in the ground. Others say that patients who die at Lier Sykehus before being sent off to be buried are returned to haunt it for eternity. Regardless, some people still visit this building to see if they can talk to these ghosts. Many then claim they have experienced something strange such as seeing shadows or hearing

The reason people say that the spirits of patients who die here return is because, in Norwegian tradition, all bodies must be buried or cremated. If you are mentally ill and die, you will be buried; otherwise, you will be cremated. There is no way for you to stay at the hospital after death, so the tradition says that the body must return to nature once it has passed away. It has also been said that if a patient dies here, they get buried at a cemetery nearby so they can rest in peace next to their relatives and loved ones.

Many people have been visiting this hospital to find ghosts or encountering haunted phenomena such as hearing voices or feeling cold spots. There are many different theories as to why people say this, like ghosts or spirits of the dead. One theory is that it is because of a haunted hospital. Still, since this hospital has been changed from what it originally was built for, many think there are just buildings that were built there, and they think people have moved into them after death or something bad happened to them in the hospital.

People also believe that when you hear footsteps at Lier Sykehus, you are not alone because a patient had died in a room downstairs. According to paranormal enthusiasts, the spirit had been stuck there for years after having committed suicide here. Yet, no one ever found evidence of anyone having died here in this room, so it could be just imagination. Other than that, people have said the sounds heard at night here are actually from people with schizophrenia or people who are hearing voices in their heads.

Many people who have come to this hospital describe voices they hear first when they come up with the check-in at the receptionist desk. They also say these voices seem to be coming from different rooms around them, like behind closed doors and on other floors. The reason for this is that when you first arrive and arrive on a floor, you should get a room close by so you can get anything you need quickly and easily. They do this because when you step on the elevator, you get the same feeling as if you are in a maze and you don't know where to go and what room to be in except on the floor that they have assigned for you. So, there is a lot of stress and anxiety from this place which can cause people to feel like they are in a maze and hear voices in their head, but it could just be old memories.

The building there is severely dilapidated. There are many parts of the building that are falling apart or about to collapse. This is because of vandalism and the fact that Lier Sykehus is just getting too old. Many people think it is haunted, and even the people who work there say they hear strange noises at night. There are also long, winding hallways that can make you feel like you are lost or don't know where to go next, adding to the paranoia and anxiety felt by many when they come here.

There have been documented ghost sightings and experiences at Lier Sykehus Hospital. The residents of Norway have reported strange activities in the hospital, as do visitors from all over the world. The hospital is located in a very rural area. There are many stories about paranormal activity, including reports of spirits, ghosts, and apparitions in common areas and patient rooms. It is believed that spirits often come down to earth to view their loved

ones or pay homage to those who have passed on.
The hospital has since been repurposed several
times, thus changing its purpose. However, the
building has been renovated a few times before, and
it is not as worn as it looks. There are many stories
about ghosts coming out of Lier Sykehus Hospital,
but there is no evidence that they are real.

10. Royal Hope Hospital

St. Augustine, Florida is the oldest permanent European settlement in the United States. With it comes a long history filled with the struggle and suffering of a developing nation. Many wars left scars on early America, especially in the south. One hospital, called Royal Hope, witnessed some of the worst of it.

Originally called Our Lady of Guadalupe, Royal Hope was first opened in St. Augustine as a Spanish military hospital, where it treated the sick and wounded from 1784-1821. It burned down but was soon replaced by an exact replica to house the wounded of the Seminole War. Historians say that at least 70% of the men who came to Royal Hope survived the hospital, but thousands found their final resting place there, given how long it was in operation.

Today, Royal Hope serves as a Spanish Military Hospital Museum, where visitors can learn more about the war and how the soldiers were treated before modern medicine. However, a discovery by St. Augustine Public Works has left people wondering what was actually going on at Royal

Hope all those years ago. Everyone knew that Royal Hope once kept a cemetery where soldiers could receive a proper Catholic burial after succumbing to their wounds. But a few years ago, workers were digging to repair plumbing near the hospital and were surprised to uncover piles and piles of human bones.

Most people figured that the historians underestimated just how big this cemetery was. However, the bones themselves suggest a different story. Why were so many bones piled together without any markers or organization? The discovery appeared much unlike a traditional Catholic burial, leaving locals to scratch their heads over what happened to all these people and wonder why their burial was kept a secret.

Rumors began to fly that the hospital had been built on an ancient Timucuan Indian burial site, a likely idea considering the area. No one was ever able to confirm this one way or another, as the bones were quickly reburied where they were found, out of respect for the dead.

Even if the bones can't speak, the ghosts of Royal Hope sure seem to. As an active museum for the war, people regularly sight strange and unexplainable things that suggest the hospital has its own story to tell. Many visitors to the sick ward have witnessed old beds and furniture moving across the room on their own—sometimes bumping into their legs as if trying to draw their attention to something.

Two tourists, in particular, spotted what they could only describe as a phantom. They claim that it appeared in front of them only long enough to look at their faces before vanishing. Could it have been the spirit of a lost soldier? No one can say. Others have reported strange sightings suggesting that the Seminole War still rages on, at least in Royal Hope.

Many have heard the distinct sound of marching footsteps coming from the upper floor of the hospital that has been vacant for decades. Anyone who went upstairs to investigate the sounds discovered nothing. More have noticed the distinct and alarming smell of sulfur, as if from gun smoke, which improbably lingers after all these years.

Other visitors to the hospital learned more than they bargained for about the despair and suffering that once permeated the building during its long history. Groans and shouts are often heard coming from otherwise empty rooms. The Prayer Room is particularly well known for these unexplainable noises. The place where dying soldiers would have received their last rights was often a place of ultimate despair.

Visitors can still feel it—describing a strange feeling of loss and helplessness when entering the room. People often hear pained groans coming from the Prayer Room, accompanied by the hushed prayers of whoever guided the soldier into the afterlife.

Passing away to the sound of soothing prayer may have been the highlight for many soldiers at Royal Hope. The strangled cries of one man can often be heard coming from the old apothecary, where workers administered pharmaceuticals to the sick. People who visit the room have reported seeing distinct shadows moving back and forth as if lost, confused, or trapped. Could they be tortured souls from a disturbing ancient burial ground, unable to find peace in death? Many wonders.

Today, the Surgeon's Office serves as a display room for the outdated and disturbing medical equipment used at the time. The equipment draws a lot of interest, especially because numerous visitors have witnessed it shaking—all on its own. Two people have also confessed that they felt someone grabbing them and their clothes, refusing to let go until they managed to rip themselves free. Maybe the doctor's still in?

They aren't the only ones who have admitted some unseen presence grabbed them. Several others have scratches to prove it on their stomachs and backs. Some of the scratches even look like they could be attempts at a message—the word 'help.' That might seem a little hard to believe. Still, the abundance of photo and video recordings of spooky, unexplainable apparitions surface every year from visitors to the hospital.

Between the mysterious piles of bones and history of needless suffering at Royal Hope, it's no wonder people are witnessing so many confusing and disturbing messages from lives long lost. Whether or not you believe everything people say about the hauntings of Royal Hope Hospital, it's clear that someone on the other side has something to say as well.

11.   The Northville State Hospital

When it first opened, the Northville Psychiatric Hospital was one of the country's largest and most "modern" psychiatric institutions. The structure was open for 51 years, from 1952 to 2003, until being demolished in 2018. The buildings housed a variety of patients with psychiatric difficulties. This institution was notorious for mistreating patients, and legend has it that patients were utilized as test subjects for doctors with more sinister motives. These horrific incidents, together with the deterioration and hazardous structure, contributed to the building's demise. The 20 buildings were distributed across 453 acres, with each serving a unique purpose for patients. Because of the tragic tragedies that occurred there, the buildings became regarded as hotspots for paranormal activity.

Although it was renamed "Northville Mental Health Center" after World War II, locals call it "the state hospital." As mental health care has changed to be more people-centered and less institutionalized, the center shifted its emphasis from outpatient treatment to care for those with chronic conditions who cannot function on their own or have no available family support system at home.

The center is housed in several buildings. The original hospital building, built in 1855, was extensively remodeled. The Thomas M. Barton Building (1910) and the District Office Building (1916) comprise three-fourths of the complex and include most administrative offices for the facility. Over the years, several other buildings have been added to accommodate varying needs.

This facility opened in 1952 and was considered one of the finest facilities in the country for treating psychiatric patients. But that reputation did not last, as reports became public decades later. Those patients were forced to sleep in hallways, were left with nothing to do but chain smoke and watch television all day, and were even subjected to attacks by staff members and other patients. Many patients were forced to eat in their cells. Patients were even beaten.

By the 1940s, Michigan's mental hospital network was overcrowded, aged, and insufficient. A new, contemporary institution was required in southeast Michigan, and Northville – previously home to a hospital for "feeble children" – was chosen. Northville State Hospital, or NSH, began construction in the mid-1940s and opened in 1952.

When it first opened, NSH was acclaimed as one of the top mental clinics in the country, with 20 buildings spread out over 453 acres of wooded, often swampy ground. Patients with differing degrees of psychological difficulties were treated in several wards and buildings throughout the campus, organized around a shining eight-story tower on the north side. The hospital was nearly self-sufficient, with its laundry, restaurant, gymnasium, movie theater, swimming pool, and bowling alley powered by a steam plant that supplied energy and heat via an underground network of tunnels.

Northville was a pioneer in using art and music as part of treatment in its early days. Patients could learn to play musical instruments, perform in plays, study mechanics or home economics, work in hospital buildings, and care for the grounds.

However, the state began to cut the mental health budget in the 1970s, eliminating several institutions and cutting services given as doctors began to rely on medicine and pharmaceuticals to treat symptoms. Crowding became a concern at Northville since the facility routinely treated over 1,000 patients despite being constructed for only 650. Some patients were forced to sleep in the gymnasium until more rooms could be made available.

Conclusion

So that brings us to the end of a one-of-a-kind collection of hauntings from abandoned hospitals around the world. I hope you learned more about these institutions' long and sometimes harsh histories. But, more importantly, I hope you were terrified!

While some of these old and haunting houses have been demolished or will be by the time this book is published, many others have been preserved for their historical importance and will be around for a long time. However, they will never have to endure the long days of caring and mistreating patients, as well as understaffing, epidemic infections, and wartime appropriation.

But whether it's faint whispers in the corridor, unexplained bouncing balls, slamming doors, probing of invisible hands, or the screams of a headless poltergeist, the spirits of these abandoned hospitals will continue to tell their tale. And as we discover more about these weird happenings through first-hand experiences, scary images, frightening films, and EVPs, more and more people will start to pay attention.

Whether or not you believe in ghosts, the fact is that any of these haunted hospitals could make for an excellent Halloween haunted house. While many of them might need a bit of work to get into proper shape, the techniques for creating a truly terrifying experience are the same in every case. I hope this book has given you some ideas and inspiration.

Next time you're feeling like a trip to the hospital, consider going on a ghost hunt instead. Who knows – you might be the one person in your group to have an actual paranormal experience. And if you do, be sure to let everyone know by sending us your story!

As always, thanks for reading, and stay safe out there!

Enjoy the haunting, and make sure to keep in touch with me. Cheers!

Matthew Clark

Most Haunted

Exorcisms and Possessions

A Scary Journey in the Most Famous True Stories of Exorcisms and Demonic Possessions

Introduction

Suppose you're into horror movies or scary stories. In that case, you'll know that the leading category in this niche is demon possession or Exorcism, in contrast to its counterpart, the zombie apocalypse, and related stories. They uniquely give you the chills that the other can't provide because of the mysterious intrigue attached to every scene and that most movies are adopted from true-life stories.

Before then, let's look at what possession and Exorcism are all about. Either it's a family or bloodline curse, you piss a voodoo priest off, or some loose spirit or demon was just having a bad day and decided to transfer aggression on whoever crossed its path. It all boils down to being possessed or taken control of by a mythical being or entity. During such periods, the victims may or may not lose consciousness and have little or no control of their bodies or coordination functions.

According to a Vatican-approved exorcist, the different signs of possession include; aversion to the sacred; so a person walks in this Church and can't look at a crucifix, and their eyes are, you only see the whites of their eyes. Another would be knowledge of hidden things, where the demon will begin to tell you something about yourself that the person would have no way of knowing. It would be followed by possessing a kind of excessive physical strength they don't normally possess. Eventually, epileptic-like seizures on a person's face and the movement of their arms and legs in a way where they lose complete control. So, if you are or know of someone experiencing such, and the person has tried medical approaches, it could be that the person is possessed.

On the other hand, Exorcism is the act of removing or expelling said demon or possessing an individual by using books, texts, and other materials that are believed to eliminate said demons.

The following cases are some real-life cases of possessions and exorcisms that have happened in the past, leaving places involved haunted and also sending chills down your spine.

1. The Exorcism of Anneliese Michel

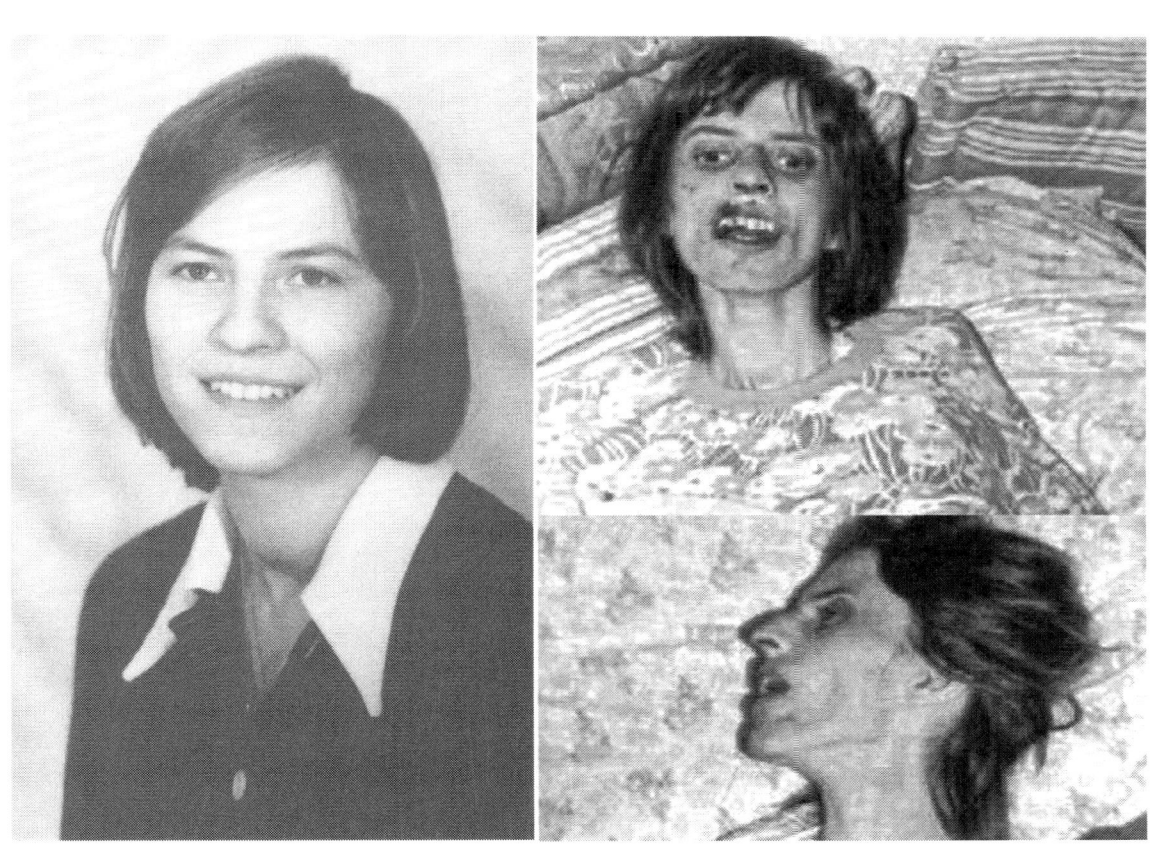

Anna Elisabeth "Anneliese" Michel (September 21, 1952 – July 1, 1976) was a German lady who died after undergoing 67 Catholic exorcism rituals in the year leading up to her death. Her parents and Priest were found guilty of negligent homicide when she died of hunger. She had been diagnosed with epileptic psychosis (temporal lobe epilepsy) and had a history of ineffective psychiatric therapy.

Anneliese Michel was born in 1952 in the small German town of Klingenberg and was raised as a strict Catholic. She was considered bright and charming. Anneliese had her first incident of falling unconscious when she was 16 years old, in September 1968. She also felt like something was pushing down on her chest, pinning her to her bed later that night. A similar incident occurred 11 months later, in August 1969. Anneliese's mother took her to their family doctor, Dr. Vogt, and a neurologist, Dr. Luthy, who examined her and even conducted an electroencephalogram, or EEG, a brain scan, discovered nothing wrong. They speculated that it could be a seizure of some sort.

Anneliese had two more similar incidents over the next three years, for which she has prescribed two medications: an anticonvulsant and an anti-seizure medicine called Dilantin. By the age of 20, she had developed an intolerance for many religious artifacts and heard voices. Despite medicine, her illness worsened, and she became suicidal and exhibited other symptoms for which she was treated. After five years of taking psychiatric drugs, Michel and her family became afraid a demon-possessed failed to alleviate her symptoms.

Things began to take a bizarre turn in the spring of 1973. In her bedroom, Anneliese began to hear knocking sounds. It sounds that her sisters would also hear. Anneliese also claimed to have heard a voice telling her she was going to hell. Anneliese's mother was even more alarmed when she saw her daughter intensely staring at a statue of the Virgin Mary with "eyes became black, jet black, and her hands seemed to morph into thick paws with claws," according to her mother.

Anneliese recounted terrifying visions of a demon face haunting her in September 1973 during a neurology visit with Dr. Luthy and stated that she believed the Devil was inside her. She also reported smelling something like burning feces, an odor that several others around her also confirmed detecting. Around this time, Anneliese's mother told Dr. Luthy about the weird incidents, and he urged them to contact a Jesuit, according to Mrs. Michel, a remark that Dr. Luthy later denied. Anneliese visited with a Freudian psychiatrist in November 1973, who described her as a neurotic with potential epilepsy. Another physician discovered she had "epileptic tendencies" and switched her from Dilantin to Tegretol, a much harsher medicine.

Anneliese's bizarre conduct increased in July 1975. She didn't get much sleep and spent the night praying earnestly. She ate spiders and flies, and she even licked the pee off the floor. On the walls, she smashed rosaries, crucifixes, and sacred pictures. Anneliese also showed "near-superhuman strength," throwing her sister "like if she were a ragdoll," and amazingly, effortlessly squeezing an apple with one hand into "fragments erupted over the room." Also, a priest named Father Rodewyk, who was regarded as an expert on exorcisms by his colleagues, said that he was sure that Anneliese was possessed and that an exorcism on Anneliese was formally allowed after consultation with the bishop.

Whether or not this is true, the family looked for a priest, and they eventually found Father Alt. When they met the Priest Ernst Alt, he told them that she "didn't appear like an epileptic' and that he didn't notice her having seizures. Alt claimed she was possessed by a demon and pleaded with the local bishop to allow an exorcism. Bishop Josef Stangl allowed the Priest Arnold Renz permission to exorcise according to the Ritual Romanum of 1614 in September of the same year, albeit with strict confidentiality. On September 24, 1975, it was to be carried out by Father Renz, a priest. Father Renz performed the first exorcism rite, and he allowed part of the exorcism sessions to be recorded, resulting in 42 audio recordings of exorcisms.

The first session was held on September 24 by Renz. Michel started talking about "dying to atone for the wayward youth of the day and the apostate priests of the modern church." Her parents stopped seeing doctors and instead relied completely on exorcism rites at this point. Over ten months in 1975–1976, 67 exorcism sessions were performed, one or two each week, lasting up to four hours.

During her sessions, Anneliese identified Fleischmann as one of her demons, providing correct details about the real Fleischmann, a priest. He was expelled from the Church for poor behavior in the 1500s. Father Alt, who believed Anneliese would have no way of knowing Fleischmann, was taken aback by these revelations.

Anneliese's behavior escalated by May when she began slamming her head against the wall and biting herself and others to the point where her family had to bind her to protect her from injuring herself. Anneliese's condition exacerbated her refusal to eat, which she described as "not being permitted to eat." Even though she was fragile and presumably weighed less than 80 pounds, she showed incredible strength when people tried to confine her.

Anneliese's entire face was sunk in by June, and she refused to see a doctor despite having a high temperature. Anneliese had another exorcism on June 30 and merely said, "Please, absolve me." Her relatives went to her room the next morning and discovered her dead.

Despite seeking medical help early on, Anneliese ultimately refused to submit to medical treatment, as she and her family put their confidence in exorcisms for the cure. After 67 exorcisms, she died of malnutrition at the age of 23. At the time of her death, she weighed barely 68 pounds.

The case was taken to court, and her family members and the other parties involved were put on trial. The defense presented eyewitness testimony and formally submitted the recordings as possession evidence, an idea that the court never seemed to take seriously. The defense argued that Anneliese was allowed to refuse medical treatment because it was her legal right, even though the medical treatment could have included tranquilization, force-feeding, and electroshock therapy. All of this is presumably done against her will. Even a family friend, Thea Hein, testified that Anneliese reportedly "begged on her knees" for Hein not to suggest medical attention to anyone in 1976, a few months before her death. However, near the end, Father Alt sought medical assistance. On May 30, his friend Dr. Richard Roth visited Anneliese out of his scientific curiosity rather than a physician.

The prosecution claimed that Anneliese had epilepsy and psychosis and that her parents and two priests were responsible for her death by failing to intervene. According to two experts, they questioned Father Alt's credibility, claiming that he showed signs of schizophrenia. The prosecution also claimed that the medications given effectively suppressed epilepsy-like seizures and that this suppression evolved into "a delusional psychosis associated with epilepsy." They claimed that Anneliese's psychosis was aggravated by the exorcisms, which only served to fuel her fantasy.

It meant that Anneliese would go through periods of normal behavior in between exorcisms. Even though she would act possessed during exorcisms, it's unclear whether Anneliese's epilepsy-like seizures were suppressed by medication or if they went away on their own, even if her psychotic visions predate the alleged medical suppression.

In the end, the court sided with the prosecution, and the four defendants were sentenced to six months in prison, suspended for three years, and ordered to pay all court costs. The court ruled that Anneliese was incapable of making her own decisions and should have been forced to undergo medical treatment.

2. The Exorcism of Anna Ecklund

Ecklund's first awareness of a feeling of disgust toward religious objects began when he was 14 years old. When she was born in Marathon, Wisconsin, and was raised as a Catholic, she could not enter churches. Something unknown seemed to hold her back. Ecklund was possessed by demons when Riesinger arrived in 1912. Because she couldn't pray or go to Church, Anna Ecklund could not receive sacraments, even though she continued to have faith. With every step she took, she heard demonic spirits whispering urgently in her ear, urging her to do terrible things. Feeling that she was losing her mind, Anna despaired. The demons returned to their previous effort levels, according to Riesinger. According to the Catholic mythos, he believed that a demonic being possessed her, and seven of his demons accompanied him. Exorcism would be much more difficult if these beings could possess humans.

Riesinger was well aware of the stakes and the potential for an exorcism to cause problems. Following the first rite, rumors circulated that Anna had been possessed due to her father Jacob's incestuous advances or that her aunt Mina had used black magic as a witch. Riesinger sought advice from his friend, Reverend Joseph Steiger of St. Joseph's parish in Earling, Iowa, because the suffering woman's soul was on the line, and there was a risk of intense local backlash. They decided to take Anna to an isolated convent run by Franciscan Sisters in Earling to ensure privacy and protection. They started making preparations for the woman's Exorcism there.

After receiving permission from the Mother Superior, the reverends brought Anna to the convent on August 17, 1928. She hissed in aversion when she smelled food that had been blessed, and she could tell when holy water had been sprinkled ahead of time. Anna was bound to an iron bed for the first of three sessions the next day to prevent any dangerous behavior. Riesinger, who has years of experience, fully expected her to attack during the ceremony. He had the convent's strongest sisters on standby to assist him.

Nothing, however, had prepared the reverends for what was about to happen. Anna sank into a deep sleep with her eyes shut tight as they said the opening prayers. She then allegedly ripped through her restraints, leaped into the air, and clung to the wall above the room's door as they officially began the exorcism rite. Theophilus had the sisters drag Anna away from the wall and into the bed, restraining her even as she howled inhumanly until the end of the first session on August 26.

Over the next two sessions, Anna quickly deteriorated from September 13 to 20 and December 15 to 23. Despite eating less and less, she vomited inexplicably large amounts during the exorcisms. Tobacco leaves and other debris seemed to make up the majority of the vomit. Anna's body began to change and distort as the demons inside her changed and distort her body physically. Her head swelled and elongated, and her face became so disfigured that few people recognized her as the humble woman who had arrived at the convent. By the end, she was a pale, deathlike figure, her body emaciated, and her eyes are glowing like red embers.

Anna's behavior changed as the Exorcism progressed. In addition to the vomit, she began to produce an uncontrollable amount of urine and feces. Anna reacted angrily to the Priest's actions, foaming at the mouth whenever Riesinger said Latin blessings. Her body even swelled to twice its normal size on one occasion, making the sisters in the room wince in fear of the woman bursting. Anna spoke in languages she had never heard before and could recall the nuns' and priests' childhood sins. After a short period, several sisters requested to leave their home for a convent with fewer problems.

They couldn't be blamed, given Anna's ongoing transformation. Her soft voice often devolved into a guttural growl capable of making unimaginable noises. Her body grew heavier, and she pressed so hard against the iron-wrought bed frame that it bent. Even while sleeping, she spoke in strange tongues, cursing God and verbally abusing anyone in the room. Anna could be brought back to her senses by blessed or holy objects, so there was still hope. The closer they got to evil Riesinger, Steiger, and the sisters, the longer they chased that hope.

Anna listed several spirits within her when asked about them, with Beelzebub as their leader. She did, however, mention that she had been possessed by her father, Jacob, and his mistress, Mina, with the assistance of Lucifer himself.

The first Exorcism had failed, according to her, because Jacob and Mina continued to poison her food with cursed spices. The pair had been cursed and had now joined Anna's demon horde. "To bring her to despair so that she will commit suicide and hang herself!" said a voice claiming to be Judas Iscariot when asked what business the spirits had with her. The Exorcism would soon be over once the demons were identified. The final session began on December 23, 1928. Anna Ecklund collapsed on her bed after standing up and screaming at the top of her lungs. When Anna's screams reached a fever pitch, an unearthly stench filled the room, and she fell silent. She blinked open her eyes. Then, for the first time in months, she spoke in a clear voice. The Exorcism was completed after 23 days, and the evil had vanished.

Ecklund was able to live a relatively peaceful existence in the years that followed. Her true identity was kept hidden from the public. Reverend Steiger was a man who lived a full life. And as more people read Begone, Satan!, the book's popularity grows. Riesinger's popularity grew. He was well-known in the Catholic community before his death in 1941, and he was featured in Time magazine in 1936.

3. The Exorcism of Roland Doe

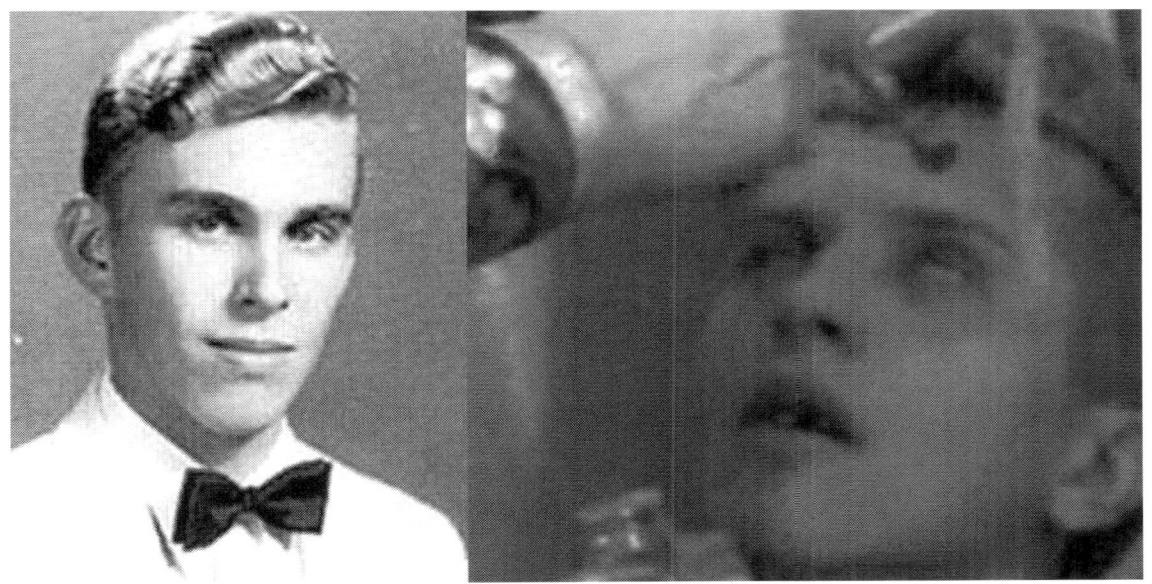

In 1949, Jesuit priests alleged they performed an exorcism in St. Louis on a boy, known pseudonymously as Roland Doe, after exhibiting signs of demonic possession after playing with an Ouija board. Roland was born into a Lutheran household in Germany. The family lived in Cottage City, Maryland, in the 1940s. Roland, according to Allen, was an only kid who relied on adults in his household for playmates, particularly his Aunt Harriet. When Roland displayed curiosity in the Ouija board, his aunt, who was a spiritualist, introduced him to it.

Before Exorcism, Roland often spoke in German and Italian dialects, which he had no prior knowledge of. During the Exorcism, Roland growled while exhibiting superhuman strength. The Exorcism was eventually performed when doctors could not find any medical explanation for the boy's actions and symptoms.

This story was presented in a documentary produced by the Catholic League and broadcast on CNN. However, the story is baseless, and few doctors even believed the story occurred. One doctor even stated that "It doesn't sound right. It sounds like a made-up story..."

Before becoming a Canon of St. Louis Cathedral, Fr. Richard Sipe interviewed one of the priests who performed the Exorcism, Frs Eugene Aull, and Roland Doe himself, and concluded that "I don't think [Roland] experienced evil spirits."

Was Roland Doe's Exorcism real or fabricated?

Despite being reported in various publications at the time and supported by several Jesuit priests and other witnesses, current skeptics have found numerous gaps in the account. What we do know is that a youngster from Cottage City, Maryland (not Mt. Rainier, Maryland, as many sources claimed), identified variously as Roland Doe and Robbie Manheim, was taken to St. Louis for treatment for troubling conduct.

Whether the disturbing behavior was caused by psychiatric disease, demonic possession, or a clever joke depends on who you believe. Many parts of the narrative, including where the youngster came from and whether he was first sent to Georgetown Hospital for treatment, proved incorrect.

While some of those could be dismissed as changes to protect the boy's identity, Opsasnick obtained quite different statements from witnesses and neighbors he interviewed.

The general agreement appears that Roland/Robbie was acting out due to emotional issues or a psychiatric episode, but nothing supernatural occurred. On the other hand, psychiatrists were more likely to see mental illness in the incidents they watched, whereas priests were more likely to see demonic possession.

There was at least one Exorcism done, according to diary reports kept by at least two priests who claim to have participated in the rituals: William S. Bowdern and Raymond J. Bishop. Both priests taught at St. Louis University, and the latter claims he found out about Roland via a classmate who happened to be the boy's cousin. Both were sure that they were in the presence of a demon in their accounts.

When author Thomas B. Allen, who published the book Possessed about Roland Doe's Exorcism, interviewed the third Priest in attendance, Thomas Halloran, he seemed to have concerns.

Where did Roland Doe's Exorcism take place?

Given the number of witnesses, it's likely that a ritual did take place in St. Louis in 1949. The boy's parents accompanied him from Maryland to Missouri, where he was treated at the university and then at The Alexian Brothers Hospital in a razed wing in 1978. The house Roland remained in with his family, on the other hand, is a popular tourist spot on Roanoke Drive and has been visited by many paranormal investigators, including the Ghost Adventures crew, over the years.

At least as of 2013, the youngster, whose name has never been revealed, appeared to be alive and in his 70s, living a regular life.

When Opsasnick found him (or thought he saw him), he didn't confirm or deny he was Roland Doe, but he made it obvious he didn't want to be interrogated about it. The priests who narrated the story have all passed away.

After the Exorcism

Following the Exorcism of "Roland Doe, his family relocated to the East. According to sources, Ronald married and established a family. He called his first child Michael after the saint who was thought to have saved his soul. Roland would be in his early 80s if he were still living today.

Following the Exorcism, the chamber at Alexian Brothers Hospital was boarded up and shut. The entire complex was demolished in 1978. After being abandoned in the 1960s, the family's home in Maryland is now an empty lot.

Experts think "Roland Doe's" true identity is Ronald Hunkeler. However, only one individual apparently knows for certain, the Priest.

4. David Berkowitz, Son of Sam Demonic Possession.

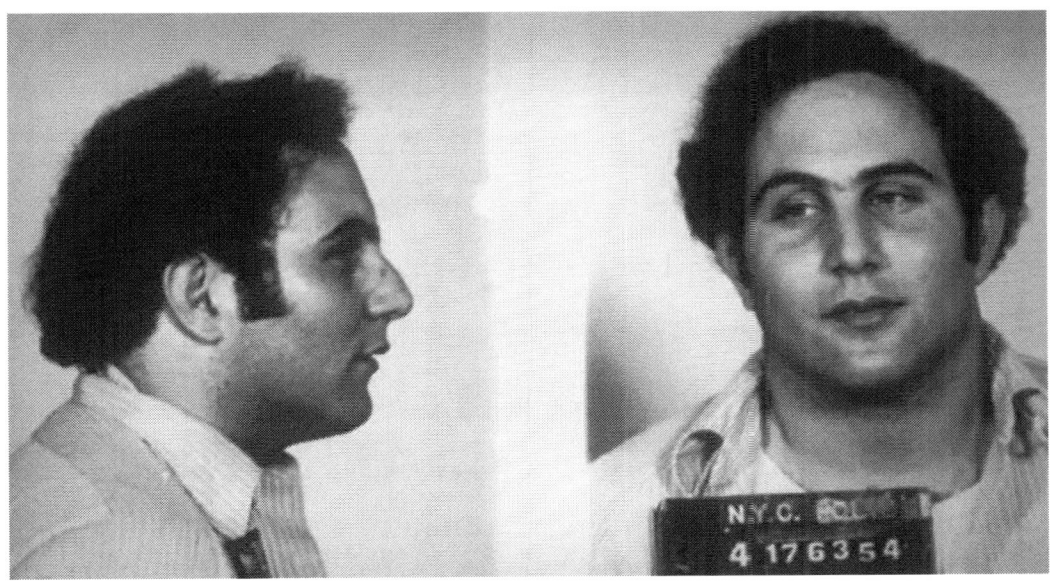

During the "Summer of Sam" in 1977, David Berkowitz shot, injured, and killed over ten people in New York City, New York. He was well-known and regarded as the personification of sin and evil. Serial killers may feel compelled to kill by an outside power larger than themselves, which can be both good and evil. These murders are performed in an attempt to fill or satisfy an emptiness in their lives, whether spiritual or not, and to overcome concerns, fears, loneliness, and insanity. David Berkowitz said that Satan drove him to conduct such heinous actions and that he was controlled and instructed to kill. He stated that his killings were not the issue but rather the way to defeating the demons that possessed him. He felt demonically possessed and sent notes marked with his tag the Son of Sam to the police and the news after his kills so that people would understand why he was doing this in the name of Satan.

David Background

David Berkowitz was raised in the Bronx by adoptive parents. He was shocked by the loss of his adopted mother from cancer in 1967, and he became increasingly isolated as a result. He entered the army in 1971 and served for three years, where he distinguished himself as a skilled marksman. He returned to New York in 1974 to work as a security guard. In 1975, his mental state worsened dramatically (he would later be diagnosed as a paranoid schizophrenic).

Feeling cut off from the rest of the world, he became an arsonist and ignited hundreds of fires in New York City without being apprehended. He began to hear voices of "demons" tormenting him and telling him to murder. On Christmas Eve 1975, he succumbed to his inner demons and badly injured 15-year-old Michelle Forman with a hunting knife.

He moved into a two-family home in Yonkers, a New York suburb, in January 1976. Berkowitz became persuaded that the German shepherd in the home and other neighboring dogs were possessed by devils who commanded him to murder attractive young ladies. During this period, one of the neighboring dogs was shot, most likely by Berkowitz. He began to perceive his neighbors as devils as well.

Berkowitz relocated to an apartment house in Yonkers in April, but his new residence also contained dogs. Berkowitz's next-door neighbor, retiree Sam Carr, owned a black Labrador dog named Harvey, whom he felt begged him to murder. He also saw Sam Carr as a strong demon and referred to him when he subsequently referred to himself as "Son of Sam."

His Attack

Berkowitz resigned from his position as a security guard on July 28, 1976. The next morning, he approached a parked automobile in the Bronx where two young ladies were conversing and fired five rounds into the vehicle with his .44 revolver. Donna Lauria, eighteen, was murdered instantaneously, and her companion Jody Valenti was injured. There were no motivations or leads in the shooting, according to police.

Berkowitz attacked again in the early hours of October 24, gravely injuring 20-year-old Carl Denaro as he sat in a vehicle in Queens, talking with a female acquaintance. On November 26, a little more than a month later, 16-year-old Donna DeMasi and 18-year-old Joanne Lomino were shot and badly injured on the street on their way home after a movie. Berkowitz fatally shot Christine Freund while she sat in a vehicle in Queens with her boyfriend on January 30, 1977. Police began to assume that a single person committed these crimes, but only a few bullets were discovered undamaged to back up their suspicions.

Virginia Voskerichian, a 19-year-old college student, was shot to death as she went home in Manhattan on March 8. A bullet was discovered undamaged, matching one discovered at the scene of Berkowitz's first murder. The New York Police Department reported the capture of a serial murderer, described as a Caucasian guy in his twenties with black hair and of average height and build.

To find the murderer, a huge squad of investigators known as the "Omega" task team was formed. Valentina Suriani, 18, and Alexander Esau, 20, were shot and murdered by the same pistol while they kissed in their parked automobile along the Hutchinson River Parkway on April 17. This time, the. The 44-caliber assassin left a message referring to himself as the Son of Sam.

Berkowitz shot Sam Carr's Labrador dog on April 29. He had already sent Mr. Carr an anonymous, threatening letter about the animal. The dog was rescued, and the Yonkers Police Department launched an investigation. Meanwhile, Berkowitz started writing strange messages to his neighbors and previous landlords. These people began to think Berkowitz was the Son of Sam and reported their concerns to local authorities. The Omega task team was alerted later, but the investigators had received hundreds of reports of Son of Sam "suspects" and were having difficulty filtering through all the dead ends.

The Son of Sam attacked again on June 26, injuring Judy Placido and Sal Lupo as they sat in their car after leaving a Queens disco. The public's fear of the rampaging serial murderer reached crisis proportions, and New York's nightclubs and restaurants witnessed a significant reduction in business. A scorching heatwave and a 25-hour blackout in mid-July only added to the angst. Berkowitz shot a young couple kissing in a parked car in Brooklyn on July 31, only two days after the anniversary of his first homicide. Stacy Moskowitz, twenty, was killed, and her boyfriend, Bobby Violante, lost his left eye and virtually all of his vision in his right eye.

A few days later, a key breakthrough in the case occurred when an eyewitness reported seeing a guy with what seemed to be a pistol minutes before the shots were fired in Brooklyn. Her information contributed to the creation of the first police sketch of Berkowitz. More importantly, she informed detectives that two police officers had issued parking fines on her street that night. Berkowitz's vehicle was finally discovered after a scan of issued tickets.

Simultaneously, Yonkers police looked into Berkowitz after he launched a harassment campaign against one of his neighbors. They alerted the Omega task group of their discoveries, convinced he was the Son of Sam. The Omega investigators eventually connected the dots, and David Berkowitz was apprehended while leaving his Yonkers home on August 10. He happily acknowledged to being Sam's son. He was carrying a semiautomatic weapon and said that he was on his way to conduct another murder. A.44-caliber revolver was also found.

There was some doubt regarding Berkowitz's mental capacity to stand trial, but on May 8, 1978, he dropped his insanity defense and pled guilty to the six murders. On the other hand, Berkowitz appeared to like the media attention his case was receiving, and he went on to sell his exclusive narrative rights to a publishing firm. This spurred New York state to enact the first of a countrywide series of so-called "Son of Sam laws," which direct the money earned by a criminal from selling their tale to a victims' compensation fund.

Berkowitz was causing harm and killing people because he believed it would release him from his possessions and obsessions. "I was once a bad guy, and I genuinely thought that Satan would come and free me," he says. He received six sentences ranging from 25 years to life in prison for the crime, which was the maximum penalty allowed at the time. He supposedly stated during his first year in prison in 1979 that he "created the Son of Sam stories so that if he ever got discovered, he could claim insanity in court." After a decade in prison, he adopted a new identity as the self-proclaimed "Son of Hope." Berkowitz believes he has been pardoned and redeemed, which means he believes he has finally overcome his demonic control. Since then, he has been denied parole. He is presently incarcerated in the Shawangunk Correctional Facility in upstate New York, where he is said to have converted to Christianity.

5. Carolyn Perron and the Perron Family

The Perron Family: father Roger, Mother Carolyn, and their five children, Andrea, Nancy, Christine, Cindy, and April, moved into the farmhouse they purchased in Harrisville, Rhode Island, in 1971. The farmhouse provided enough space for them to raise their five kids. They had no idea what would happen throughout the decade they stayed there. When they moved in, the former owners only gave them one piece of advice: "For the sake of your family, leave the lights on at night!" While they were perplexed by the comment at first, it wouldn't be long before they followed the advice.

The Perrons lived in the house for several years, gradually uncovering its history and the numerous prior residents who had died there. While their findings were bleak, Roger and Carolyn may have accepted the house's darker days if it hadn't been for the spirits that lingered in the house long after they died.

In the Winter of 1971, The Perron Family decided that a tranquil life in the country was in order. Roger and Carolyn moved into a big, ten-bedroom mansion in Harrisville, Rhode Island, with their five kids. The mansion, known as The Old Arnold Estate, was completed in 1736 and lay on 200 acres of land. Almost soon, paranormal activity began. The girls became aware of a small guy roaming about the house. He frequently moved their toys around behind their backs, unnoticed. Carolyn, too, began to realize that someone or something was moving the broom. She would occasionally hear the sound of the broom's bristles scratching across the kitchen tile. When she went and returned, she would frequently discover a little amount of dirt in the center of the floor.

Another ghost gradually revealed itself to the Perron sisters. A guy with a crooked smile would emerge in the corners of their room, observing the girls play. They began to call this ghost Manny. Roger and Carolyn would have been hard pushed to believe the girls' crazy claims were genuine if they hadn't seen the ghosts for themselves.

Other weird occurrences began to happen soon after. Beds would occasionally float a few inches above the ground. Furniture looked to have their own thoughts, sliding over the floors on their own.

As picture frames often fell off the walls, doors would open and bang shut. Roger and Carolyn gradually learned more about the house's history, which was far worse than they could have anticipated.

Prior to the Perron family, eight generations had resided on the Arnold Estate, and many of them had met with tragic ends. Mrs. John Arnold, the family's ninety-three-year-old matriarch, hanged herself in the property's barn in the late 18th century. She was only one of several suicides that occurred on the property. Prudence Arnold, eleven, was raped and killed in the house by a farmhand, while her relative, Johnny, committed suicide by hanging himself in the attic. There were also two drownings in a stream that flowed through the estate throughout the years, as well as the deaths of four men who inexplicably froze on the grounds some years earlier.

Despite this bleak past, the Perron family found solace in the fact that all of the ghosts they had encountered in the home had been helpful. That is, until the other spirits of Arnold Estate made their presence known.

Late at night, the girls saw an unwanted visitor in their beds. While they slept, an unseen entity would tug on their legs and hair. One spirit began to torture Cindy, eight, by repeatedly telling her that there were dead soldiers buried in the walls.

There is one ghost that the Perron family refuses to discuss in great detail, despite all of the family's otherworldly encounters. Andrea Perron, who published a book about her family's experiences in the house, suggested that the ghost assaulted her and her sisters. That apparition, however, was not the only bad ghost that stayed in the house. The Arnold Estate was plagued by a spirit known as Bathsheba.

According to local tradition, Bathsheba Thayer married Judson Sherman in the mid-1800s and later moved to the Old Arnold Estate. Bathsheba was charged with murder when the union's first child died. A sharp instrument had impaled the infant's skull, and the townspeople murmured that the murder had been committed as a sacrifice to Satan, and that Bathsheba was a practicing Satanist who had summoned the Devil to bestow her the gift of beauty. She was detained but released soon after owing to a lack of evidence. She remained in the house for the rest of her life as an outcast from the town, dying in the early twentieth century by hanging herself from a tree behind the house. Her body is reported to have magically turned to stone after she died.

Bathsheba and her husband did, in fact, dwell in the house, according to public record. She was also implicated in the death of her neighbor's baby child, who had been left in her care, though no trial was ever held. Bathsheba and Judson Sherman died in the 1880s and spent their final years at the old Arnold Estate. She was laid to rest in a local Baptist cemetery, where her gravestone may still be located.

Bathsheba's specter, on the other hand, loomed big for the Perron family. They were sure that her malevolent soul lingered on the land, intent on tormenting anybody who set foot on it. Every member of the Perron family saw her, her face gray and her head twisted to one side as if her neck had been permanently broken. Nonetheless, it became obvious that the creature was particularly interested in Carolyn, her least favorite person in the home.

Initially, these assaults were minor. Carolyn felt small pinches on her flesh or was smacked by an unidentified hand. Bathsheba began to hurl various items at Carolyn anytime she was caught off guard. However, things continued to deteriorate. Carolyn was sitting on the couch one day when a searing ache went up to her leg. She checked herself and discovered a puncture hole on her leg that was already bleeding. The wound appeared to have been caused by a sewing needle. Bathsheba attempted to possess Carolyn when these attacks failed to get her to leave the residence.

Roger Perron and his daughters were desperate for assistance and called Ed and Lorraine Warren. The famed paranormal investigators were already well-known for their work on instances such as the infamous Amityville house haunting. Carolyn was tossed around the room like a ragdoll, and the

Warrens and Perrons stared in terror as she talked to them in a foreign voice. The Warrens decided to provide a hand and set out to rid the house of all evil.

Later on, the Perrons desired nothing more than to leave Arnold Estate, but they could not do so due to financial difficulties. They suffered the number of ghosts in the house for ten long years until they were financially able to move in 1980. Today, paranormal enthusiasts are kindly urged to respect the present owners' privacy and stay away from the property; perhaps they are afraid of reawakening the ghosts.

6. The Defeo Family (Amityville Horror)

This is nearly completely due to the 1977 novel The Amityville Horror, subsequently adapted into a film series. Despite the book's claim that it recounts the "actual narrative" of the hauntings that occurred within its walls, there is evidence that the inhabitants of 112 Ocean Avenue – George and Kathy Lutz – made up the story that became an urban legend.

The horrific killings that occurred in the mansion before the Lutz's tenancy, on the other hand, were not manufactured. Six members of the DeFeo family were murdered in their sleep with a .35 caliber rifle on November 13, 1974.

Ronald "Butch" DeFeo Jr., the eldest kid, admitted to murdering his whole family in cold blood at 23. Louise and Ronald DeFeo Sr. and his siblings 18-year-old Dawn, 13-year-old Allison, 12-year-old Marc, and nine-year-old John Matthew were all killed.

The heinous Amityville killings are thought to have triggered the spirits that haunt 112 Ocean Avenue.

Some claim, however, that the DeFeo family was also a victim of the home.

So, did an evil presence already inhabit the home before the Amityville killings, compelling a young man to murder his whole family?

Ronald DeFeo Jr.'s upbringing was financially secure but not content. His father was a dominating and abusive guy, and his mother seemed to recede into the background due to his dominant nature. Ronald DeFeo Jr. became increasingly disturbed as he matured into his adolescence. To cope, he began to rely on narcotics and booze. He retaliated aggressively and threatened his father with a pistol. DeFeo's parents believed that a weekly stipend and gifts would satisfy their difficult son. Ronald had a job at the family-owned auto business at 18, but he rarely showed there.

So it was not unusual for DeFeo to leave work at noon on that day in 1974 out of boredom. He went to a pub with pals, continually phoning his house, getting no answer, and whining to anybody who would listen. Eventually, he departed. The next time anybody saw Ronnie, Amityville would be permanently changed.

According to Valrie Plaza's book, DeFeo returned to the bar about 6:30 a.m., shouting, "You had to assist me!" "I believe my mum and father have been assassinated!" Some customers followed him back to the residence on Ocean Avenue, where they witnessed the terrible sight inside.

All six victims were discovered in their beds, on their stomachs. At about 3:15 a.m., the victims seemed to have been shot with a high-powered rifle. The victim is Ronald Jr.'s parents, Ronald DeFeo Sr. and Louise DeFeo, as well as his four siblings, Dawn, Allison, Marc, and John Matthew, who were killed. All of the victims were shot about three o'clock in the morning using a .35 caliber lever action Marlin 336C rifle. Both DeFeo's parents had been shot twice, while all of the children had been murdered with single shots. According to physical evidence, Louise DeFeo and her daughter Allison were both conscious at the time of their deaths. The victims were discovered face down in bed, according to Suffolk County Police. The DeFeo family had owned 112 Ocean Avenue since 1965. The six victims were eventually interred at Farmingdale's Saint Charles Cemetery.

However, there were a few things that didn't makeup. There were no indications of a fight or proof that they had been drugged on the corpses. No waking neighbors reported hearing any gunshots, only the DeFeo family dog barking into the night. Following an inquiry, Ronald DeFeo's alibi of being at work and then the bar began to crack, as investigators discovered the family had died before 6 a.m. DeFeo hurriedly altered his narrative, as he did numerous times throughout the inquiry into the Amityville killings.

At one point, he claimed that mob hitman Louis Falini murdered his family and forced DeFeo to see it. However, Falini had a good out-of-state alibi, and

DeFeo quickly confessed to police what was thought to be the truth: he murdered his family on his own.

On October 14, 1975, DeFeo went on trial. His attorney, William Weber, filed an insanity plea on his behalf, claiming that the defendant heard voices telling him to kill his family.

On the other hand, the prosecution contended that while the drug-addicted DeFeo was disturbed, he understood exactly what he was doing when he committed the Amityville murders. A jury found him guilty on six counts of second-degree murder and sentenced him to six consecutive terms ranging from 25 years to life in prison.

In a later version of Ronald DeFeo Jr.'s altered narrative, he claims that his sister Dawn murdered their father, and then their heartbroken mother murdered all of the siblings. DeFeo only killed his mother in this scenario. Then, in another version told by DeFeo in 1990, Dawn shoots all the DeFeos before he kills Dawn. Other hypotheses suggest that there was a second gunman in the house.

Though the legends of the Amityville house being haunted are debatable, there is considerable doubt that Ronald DeFeo Jr. was there for his family's horrific murder at the house. But the question of whether the Amityville home is indeed haunted remains unanswered.

Whether you think the Amityville home is haunted or not, there is still some intriguing material available. Daniel Lutz, one of their kids, claimed to have possessed a spirit similar to Regan MacNeil in The Exorcist. Their second son, Christopher, is adamant that he has had encounters with the paranormal, including a time when he saw a presence "as definite as a shadow" in the figure of a man that walked toward him and then vanished.

Surprisingly, both George and Kathy Lutz passed a lie detector exam concerning their tale.

7. Exorcism of Michael Taylor

Michael Taylor (born about 1944) rose to prominence in England in 1974 due to the Ossett murder case and his purported demonic possession. The case received significant coverage in the British media. Although some contend that he was not possessed, Taylor was sent to a mental institution because his wicked intentions were not hallucinatory.

Taylor worked as a butcher in Ossett, West Yorkshire. Taylor's wife, Christine, told a Christian Fellowship Group to which Taylor joined in 1974 that his connection with the group's lay leader, Marie Robinson, was "carnal." Robinson herself told the group that Taylor was a "satanist," and he was excommunicated from the group in October 1976. On November 1, 1973, Taylor was convicted of assaulting his wife with an iron bar. He served only nine months of his sentence after claiming that his wife had attacked him first.

Taylor began to attend an evangelical Christian Bible study group at Ossett Baptist Church run by Marie Robinson in 1974 and began working with Robinson in her telemarketing business, Joseph

Enterprises Ltd., at Ossett in 1976. Michael Taylor acknowledged to feeling wicked within himself and finally verbally assaulted Robinson, who shouted back at him. Michael Taylor obtained an absolution at the following meeting, but his behavior proceeded to become increasingly unpredictable. Consequently, the local vicar summoned other ministers skilled in deliverance to cast out the demons dwelling within the guy.

The Exorcism, which took place on the 5–6 October 1974 at St. Thomas's Church in Gawber, was led by Father Peter Vincent, the Anglican Priest of St. Thomas's, and assisted by the Rev. Raymond Smith, a Methodist clergyman. The Exorcism was recorded on videotape, with the explicit permission and encouragement of Michael Taylor. The tape is now in possession of Michael Taylor's family (and has been digitized).

Exorcism was successful in that it apparently drove the possessing entity away. After the Exorcism, Michael Taylor returned to work and lived a relatively normal life. He retired in December 1991, after which re-emergence of symptoms led to his being committed to a mental hospital in 1992, where he remained until his death early in 1998 (the actual date is unclear). Father Michael Maginot performed the last Exorcism on August 24 1995.According to Bill Ellis, a modern cultural expert on folklore and the occult, the exorcists thought they had: "During an all-night ritual, at least forty demons, including those of incest, bestiality, blasphemy, and lewdness, were called and cast out. Finally, weary, they let Taylor go home, despite their belief that at least three devils remained in him: insanity, murder, and violence."

Michael Taylor viciously murdered his wife, Christine, when she was at home. He assaulted her with his bare hands, pulling out her eyes and tongue and nearly ripping her face off, before murdering their dog. A police officer discovered him nude in the street, covered in blood.

Taylor was acquitted on the basis of insanity in his March trial. He was committed to Broadmoor Hospital for two years before being transferred to a security ward in Bradford for another two years before being freed. The unusual character of the case drew a lot of attention.

Taylor made headlines again in July 2005 after being convicted guilty of indecently touching a teenage girl. A week into his jail sentence for the killing, Taylor – who had tried suicide four times in the years before the conviction – resumed showing the odd behavior that had preceded his wife's death in 1974. When he was brought back before the court, they ordered him to get psychiatric treatment once more.

8. Exorcism of Clara Germana Cele

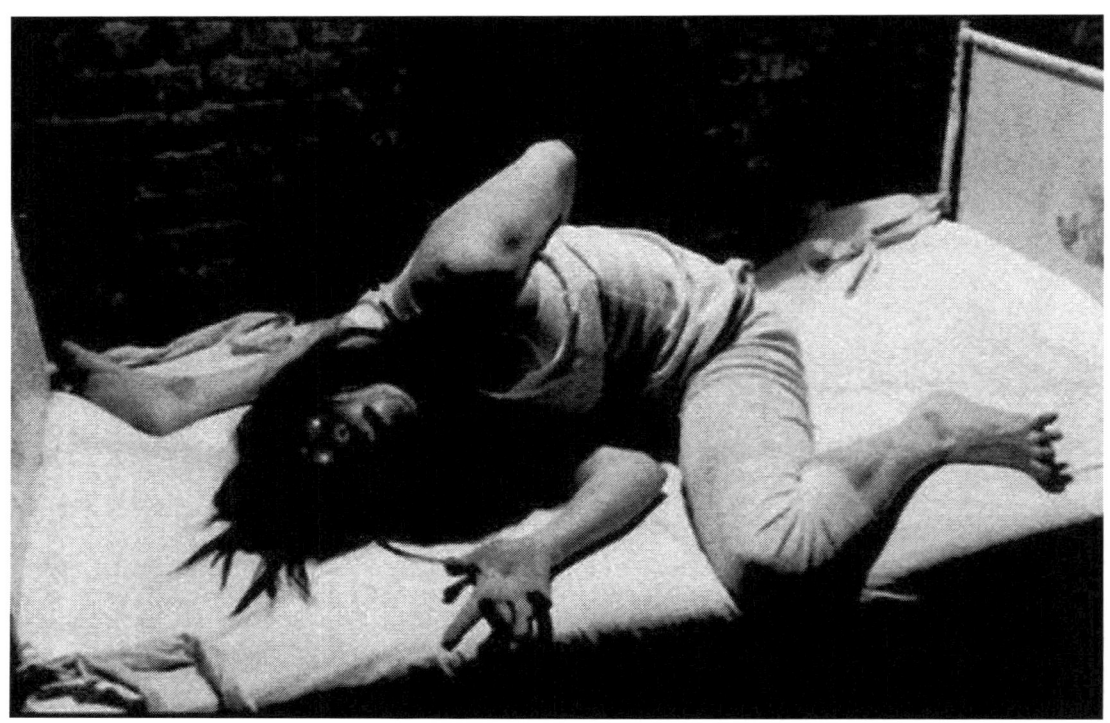

Clara Germana Cele was 16 years old when she was discovered to be possessed by an evil spirit. It is strongly suspected that he previously made a pact with the spirit. Clara was an orphan of African descent who had been baptized as a child. The girl made a pact with Satan when she was sixteen, which is the cause of her demonic possession. Clara later told her confessor, Father Hörner Erasmus, about this knowledge. According to a nun's account, Clara was said to be able to speak languages she had never heard of before. Others attest that she "understood Polish, German, French, Norwegian, and all other languages." According to the nun, Clara exhibited clairvoyance by revealing the most intimate secrets and transgressions of people she had no contact with.

Furthermore, Clara was unable to tolerate the presence of blessed objects and appeared to be imbued with extraordinary strength and ferocity, frequently hurling nuns around the convent rooms and beating them up. According to the nun, the girl's cries had a savage bestiality that astounded those around her.

According to all accounts, Clara was a very normal, even shy kid who was as devout and pious as her friends. There would have been no sign at the time that anything was wrong with her, or that evil forces were gathering about her like storm clouds on a bright day, and certainly, no indication that this beautiful young girl would go on to become one of the scariest demonic possession cases on record.

The majority of what is known about the case comes from notebooks and diaries written by nuns and priests at the mission. While it is unknown when the episode began, it appears likely that it began with a confession Clara made one day. She supposedly informed her confessor, Father Hörner Erasmus, that she had called out to the Devil to establish a dark alliance, but she did not elaborate on why she had done so. However, soon following this revelation, a sequence of odd events would begin to orbit the girl.

Clara, who knew no other languages, began to talk in Polish, German, French, Latin, and other languages, beginning with a few words here and there and then progressing to complete phrases and even raving. She had never shown any talent or even an interest in these languages, leaving everyone confused and a bit concerned that she should now know them to any degree. Clara, too, said she had no idea how she was able to speak these languages. Many others at the mission observed this. It was also stated that these periods of speaking foreign languages frequently occurred after Clara fell into a type of stupor or trance. She would sometimes not even recall what she had spoken of what had happened to her during these spells.

Soon after, Clara progressed to impulsively spewing forth the deepest, darkest secrets of others around her, including horrible things they had done and dirty thoughts they had had. She reveled in the most heinous sexual fantasies she said the members of the cloth around her had, many of which were corroborated in journal entries by terrified nuns who believed Clara could read their minds. She seemed to know all of their concerns and numerous other bits of knowledge she had no right to know, and it was at this time, everyone realized something very weird was going on.

Clara began to develop an aversion to religious images in the days that followed, which must have been difficult given that she was on a Christian mission. She would take circuitous routes around these things and couldn't stand being in the same room with them.

During these episodes, it was reported that Clara would gain tremendous strength, toss nuns across the room, and be unable to be restrained even by four people. Clara's overall propensity to progressively shift from a previously quiet and even shy adolescent to a more assertive, strong, and combative personality corresponded with this. She would hiss, snarl, and growl at everyone around her, most of the time unprovoked, and the increasingly terrified nuns sought assistance in performing an exorcism on what they were now sure was a demon-possessed kid.

Rev. Mansueti and Rev. Erasmus, two Roman Catholic priests, went about executing an exorcism on Clara, which proved to be a frightening ordeal. When faced with the two, the girl sprang onto Rev. Mansueti, knocked away his bible, and began strangling him with his stole, and she would have succeeded if a group of nuns and the other Priest hadn't pulled her off of him. After that, she started throwing items around and allegedly levitated a full 5 feet of the floor, forcing those there to have her restrained.

For two days, the priests faced whatever demonic evil was living within Clara. During it all, she demonstrated numerous characteristics that convinced everyone there that she was not just a mentally sick kid or crazy. She seemed to know when she was being sprayed with holy water, in addition to levitation and speaking in tongues. To put this to the test, the priests swapped between holy water and plain water without Clara's knowledge, but while regular water had no impact, holy water drove her insane. However, it appears that the holy water was the key, which ultimately threw the demon out.

The case is obscure and poorly recorded, yet it is unquestionably strange and was observed by many individuals. Various witnesses saw this teenager exhibit classic signs of demonic possession, including speaking in languages they have no business knowing, aversion to religious paraphernalia, superhuman strength, uncharacteristic violent behavior if the reports are to be believed. According to some, the girl levitated five feet in the air, sometimes vertically, sometimes horizontally; when sprinkled with holy water, she is claimed to have come out of her diabolical possession. They may all be telling the truth, but why would they? How can one explain these events if they are caused by mental illness? There is no way of knowing if demonic possession is true in the literal sense, but the case of Clara Germana Cele undoubtedly rates among the most potentially authentic reports available.

According to a Lutheran Pastoral Handbook, these signs indicate that a person is possessed rather than suffering from a mental disease. As a result, two Roman Catholic priests, Rev. Mansueti (Director of the St. Michael's Mission) and Rev. Erasmus (her confessor) were assigned to execute an exorcism on Clara Germana Cele lasted two days. Clara's initial move during the Exorcism was to knock the Holy Bible from the Priest's hands and grasp his stole to suffocate him with it. The Devil was claimed to have been pushed out of the girl at the end of the Exorcism.

9. The Smurl's Poltergeist

The Smurls went through hell and pure torture that no human being should have to endure. In 1972, there was a terrible hurricane that came through called hurricane Agnes. It flooded many people out of their homes, and among them were Jack and Janet Smurl. They had several children and a pet German Shepherd by the name of Simon. Because of the flood, they had to look for another place to live, and that is how they moved into a that was located at 328 chase Street in West Pitts in Pennsylvania.

They moved into the home in 1973 with their parents, so Jack's parents, by the name of John and Mary, moved to the other side of the duplex. A duplex is a house that's kind of split into two so that people can live on one side some people can live on the other. It's similar to an apartment, but it looks like a normal house. So, Jack's family, John and Mary Smurl, moved into one side of the duplex while Jack and Janet moved into the other half with their children.

There were no issues for the first 18 months of living in the house; everything was completely fine.

Though there were few occurrences here and there that had happened, but not enough to call it paranormal or cause scare to the point of making you want to move out. Though, some of the happenings at that time were a little bit odd. Since the house was built in 1896, it was backdated for the Smurfs, so they began renovating the duplex themselves, installing new floors, and doing many paintings to make it a little bit modern. But, little did they know that the next thirteen years were going to be the worst period of their lives, all because of their new home. The beginning of 1974 was like any other year until strange noises, and other odd occurrences began to disrupt the peace. As time passed, the cases became severe, and they began to experience things like the television and water pipes getting destroyed without anyone actually doing it. Later on, they started seeing apparitions and continued for the next 11 years, with each week getting worse and worse.

When the paranormal occurrences began to change rapidly for the Smurls, really dark, violent things started happening there. Initially, they kept it secret and didn't come out about it for several years to come, but everything got so bad that they ended up actually coming out to the public about it in the 80s in an effort to seek help. By that time, they were scared for their lives; the darkest of things you could imagine occurs in a haunted house was what was happening there. In the summer of 1986, the family decided to come public about what had been happening in their home since 1974.

The haunted attacks: Let's begin with a very large ceiling fan falling from their ceiling randomly and almost landing on one of their daughters, Shannon, and almost killing her. They were all excited about going to the Church for their daughter's confirmation rite when the fan above started to shake, tore itself loose, and almost hit the girl. After this incidence came to the ghostly attacks and disturbances of which they were repeatedly attacked by what they believe to be a demonic entity inside of their home. One of the daughters said that she would be lying in her bed on repeated occasions, and she could actually see what looked like people, really creepy people floating in her bedroom like above her bed, while she was trying to sleep.

Not long after that, the odor came; they started smelling something terrible in their house almost constantly and related the odor to that of rotten flesh. They said it was horrible sometimes, you wouldn't smell anything, and then suddenly, this wave of rotten flesh would just overtake their entire house. It was all that they could smell (Imagine if you were about to dig into your favorite meal, and that happened). The ghostly attacks got so bad that there was one night that Janet and Jack were actually intimate in their bedroom, and Janet was violently pushed off of her bed in the middle of the activity with her husband. He was left on the bed by himself, gagging from the smell. I'd say that that's some jealous ghost.

That wasn't the first time somebody was physically lifted up and thrown or levitated off something. It was claimed that they were levitated off of their beds on multiple occasions and even said that their dog, Simon, was picked up and thrown into a wall. Jack said that there was one night that he was praying.

There had been a lot of activity in the house that night, and he was actually pulled off the bed and dragged across the floor

The slaps: Still on the ghost attacks, several family members in this house got slapped by absolutely nothing. They felt as if a hand hit them and said that sometimes when they would feel this and turn around to see what it was, they would see these dark shadows just hovering around. This happened multiple times, and it wasn't like a random slap and not finding out who did it. It happened to many people in the family several times, and it was always accompanied by this just really dark shadow.

Electricity and plumbing problems: prior to the ghosts, the lights would turn on and off, doors would open and close, drawers would even open and close. They said that one of their TVs actually burst into flames, among other electrical problems. They also had many problems with their pipes since they were remodeling the house; their toilets would randomly flush by themselves. There were animal claw-like scratches on the bathtubs and so on. On multiple occasions, they would hear what sounded like somebody scratching violently on the walls or on the floor, even if no one was there. They also heard their names being called on several occasions, like when one of their daughters, Janet, would go down into the basement to do the wash and she heard somebody who sounded like their mother calling "Janet, Janet..." and she would reply only to realize that she wasn't there.

After a decade of psychological torture, the family called Annette and Lorraine Warren. By then, the Warrens were already known for their work. Their investigation led to an obvious conclusion there were lots of evil presences, but one demon was in control, and what was most frightening was the fact that a passageway between two dimensions was located in the house. This could be the reason for the haunting. The Warrens tried everything from exorcisms to antagonizing whatever was there, but nothing seems to work. The house was now under full possession, with people being constantly attacked violently, intensifying every time the family was starting to lose hope and thought they were doomed to live in damnation. But, after the fourth and final Exorcism, things became better after moving out of the residence, and the family had complete relief in 1986. The peace they had experienced so long ago had finally returned to them; however, the family would never be the same again.

10. The Tanacu Exorcism of Maricica Irina Cornici

Maricica Irina Cornici, a supposedly mentally ill nun from the Romanian Orthodox Church of Tanacu in the County of Vaslui, Romania, was declared murdered by the Exorcism led by Priest Daniel Petre Corogeanu and four Orthodox Christian nuns of the Holy Trinity order. The story was widely reported in Romanian media. Following a long trial, the Priest was sentenced to seven years in appeal, one nun to six, and another three nuns to five years. However, many of the locals of Tanacu, including Cornici's brother, felt she had suffered from demonic possession. The coroner Dan Gheorghiu claimed that an overdose of adrenaline in the ambulance caused the nun's death.

Maricica Irina Cornici, 23, moved to the Tanacu Monastery in January 2005. She was born into a broken home. She and her brother grew up in the orphanage following the suicide of her father. When she was 19, she worked in Germany as a nanny, then in Banat for a family. An orphanage friend of hers became a nun in the Tanacu monastery, who encouraged her to become a nun too. She started chuckling at Mass shortly after, and by April, her mental state had deteriorated to the point where doctors at the local psychiatric institution diagnosed her with schizophrenia. After two weeks of therapy, she was released into the monastery care. Cornici's friends reportedly claimed she never showed signs of mental illness. Her brother testified that he was with her when he saw Satan going "to her" and said she had been diabolically possessed.

Daniel Petre Corogeanu was the monastery's 29-year-old Priest. A decade before the events, in Vaslui, his native town, he was a soccer player. After being denied admittance to the University of Bucharest, where he planned to study sports or law, he began theological studies at the University of Iași. One year later, a businessman recruited him from his hometown to help establish a monastery bordering the town. He had been ordained by the local bishop, who expected his studies to continue. However, he gave up his academic study to dedicate himself to the administration of the monastery.

Father Corogeanu had differences with the diocese in 2003. When the bishop came to read him the law of the Canon, he contended that the Freemasonry regulations were "innovations of the 19th century." The initial community of monks disbanded as they became priests and, instead, Corogeanu created a community of religious nuns "totally devoted to him," according to all reports.

Father Corogeanu believed that Cornici was possessed by Satan, not only a mental condition. He further claimed that "the devil can't be taken out of humans with medications," so Exorcism existed. To prevent her from violent movements, including those that struck her, she was confined by the nuns in her bedroom as they took part in the ritual of the Ascension of Jesus. A few days later, with their arms held out, they bound her to a cross and took her inside the Church to anoint her. According to Sr. Nicoleta Arcalianu, Cornici was confined in the same way as others possessed by demons; Sr. Arcalianus added that if she hadn't restrained Cornici, she 'might have murdered herself or killed anyone else.' Sister Arcalianu said, with relation to Cornici, 'Irina knew she had evil spirits since she asked us to tie her together and help her.'

Her wrists and forehead were then salvaged with holy oil and remained three days in the Church. They placed a cloth in her mouth that prevented her from cursing and prayed to throw the Devil out as they bathed her lips with holy water. Cornici was then taken and untied in her room. According to Father Corogeanu, she was "healed." Later on, she had bread and tea and fainted after she had eaten. The nuns couldn't get her up and felt her pulse was faint and phoned an ambulance. She was given six doses of adrenaline in the ambulance, but she was dead when she arrived at the hospital.

The hospital doctors contacted the police, who saw the marks left by the shackles on both wrists and knees. An autopsy from 2005 claimed that she died of dehydration, tiredness, and oxygen deficiency.

Father Corogeanu and the four religious who supported him were accused of murder and the deprivation of freedom. The Prosecutors sought a life sentence for Corogeanu but were convicted to 14 years imprisonment in 2007 and 5-8 years' imprisonment on the nuns (Nicoleta Arcalianu, Adina Cepraga, Elena Otel, and Simona Bandanas).

Many people were present in the courtroom to support Father Corogeanu and were disturbed by the judgment. The Court of Appeal decreased his sentence to 7 years, and in November 2011, Corogeanu was released after completing two-thirds of his sentence.

During Marice Irina Cornici's burial, "the claps of thunder were heard," and Corogeanu concluded, "that the will of God was done."

The monastery was closed down by the Romanian Orthodox Church, and Corogeanuwas excommunicated.

However, it was discovered in 2014 that the cause of death was due to an overdose of adrenaline administered in the ambulance; as Coroner Dan Gheorghiustated, 'I was a member of the team in charge of the exhumation of the nun's body.' The conclusion was that an excess of adrenaline killed the woman. Don't ask me, and I don't know why the judges didn't consider it." According to Fr. Corogeanu, "My biggest blunder was calling an ambulance when I noticed she wasn't moving. I suppose she is dead because she was given too much adrenaline by the doctors who came with the ambulance. If I didn't call the ambulance, she'd be OK now."

In Tanacu, many people still claim that Cornici was possessed rather than mentally ill, and Corogeanu did his best to help her. Veronica Tomulescu said, "It's not like they killed her. They didn't stab her or shoot her. They took her alive to the hospital."

11.   Nicole Aubrey's Possession

Nicole Aubrey (sometimes spelt Obry) was a married young girl who began experiencing bodily torments in November 1565, which she said were caused by a vision of her deceased grandfather. Nicole, a fifteen-year-old resident of Vervins, France, had gotten so ill that she couldn't eat and allegedly went into such contortions that, as one eyewitness subsequently described, twelve or fifteen men were required to hold her down. She also talked in a harsh and scary tone, claiming that her grandfather's ghost controlled her. The grandpa said that he died without confessing and that as a result, Nicole and her family were required to perform different penances. Despite the family's efforts to comply, the possession persisted.

Nicole's family arranged for an exorcism to be performed by a Dominican priest, Pierre de la Motte. De la Motte persuaded the possessed spirit that it was a devil rather than an angel through numerous exorcisms. Nicole's possession worsened, and she became deaf, blind, and deafeningly (to make her unable to take communion). In addition, the principal devil who possessed her allegedly encouraged a slew of other devils to come in and inhabit her body. According to accounts, de la Motte expelled twenty-eight of Nicole's demons, following which they "fled to Geneva" (which was the centre of the Calvinist movement at the time). The principal demon that possessed her called himself "Beelzebub, the Prince of the Huguenots". Huguenots were French Protestants), insisted that no one could force him out save the Bishop of Laon. When Bishop Jean de Bours came to Vervins in January 1566 to perform an exorcism, he had no better luck than the other priests.

The issue rapidly became political, with local Huguenots arguing that the entire possession tale was a fabrication and attempting to halt the exorcisms. They had cause to be sceptical, given that "Beelzebub" was accusing them of collaborating with Satan. Nicole was transported to Laon, mostly for her own safety, where she was subjected to a series of public exorcisms with all the grandeur of a religious spectacle. Nicole was carried in a huge religious procession from the monastery where she resided to the beautiful Cathedral Notre-Dame de

Laon, where she ascended a specially built scaffold. The exorcist would instruct "Prince Beelzebub" to appear in front of a huge crowd, and Nicole would obediently deliver a lecture on the atrocities that the Protestants would wreak on France's Catholics. The substance was like the anti-Huguenot sermons delivered regularly by priests and bishops across the country.

The fact that a demon, one of Satan's fallen angels, was telling Catholics who were hearing what they most wanted to believe about their Huguenot neighbours seemed certain to exacerbate religious tensions. "Prince Beelzebub," told his audience, among other things, that local Huguenots had taken a communion wafer, sliced it up, and burnt the fragments. "Beelzebub" also bragged, "I will do Him [Christ] more damage than the Jews did!"

"The Catholics in great pleasure offered praises to God, being more confirmed in their faith," one Catholic chronicler wrote of Nicole Aubrey's public exorcisms. "While some Huguenots returned to the road of salvation, others became more and more obstinate, ridiculing the entire ensuing affair." The fact that Huguenots maintained that the entire event was a deception performed by the Church employing a naïve little girl did nothing to alleviate tensions. The "miracle of Laon" happened on February 8, 1566, when the Bishop of Laon held up a communion wafer and drove out the last of Nicole's demons. Nicole appears to have slipped into obscurity after that since nothing further appears to have been documented about her.

The "miracle" of Laon helped to cement anti-Protestant views, with Catholic clergy disseminating the news across Europe to become one of the Counter-rallying Reformation's grounds. It was also crucial in the religious holy wars that raged in France throughout the 16th century. This includes the St. Bartholomew's Day Massacre in August 1572, which resulted in the deaths of thousands of Huguenots. The French Wars of Religion would last until the end of the 16th century, culminating in the expulsion of the Huguenots from France.

One of the most interesting aspects of Nicole's possession was her ability to communicate without the use of her vocal cords. Jean Boulaese, the author of the most well-known account of Nicole and her possession:

Speaking in Nicole, with her mouth open wide enough to allow a walnut to pass through and swelling beneath the throat; or, to be more precise, beneath the chin; but in any case, without using or moving the lips, the grandfather replied loudly in a cracked voice: I am from God, who endured death and suffering for us all, from the virgin Mary, and all the saints of Pentecost. I am Joachim Willot's soul.

Nicole first maintained that her grandfather's spirit was using her body with her conscious participation, but she was subsequently obliged to alter this to conform to Catholic theology. Because theology did not permit the idea of "good spirits" using living humans to transmit messages, their interrogation moulded her replies to conform with Church teachings on demonic possession. Given her eagerness to please her interrogators, the anti-Protestant message she conveyed does not come as a surprise.

Nicole Aubrey's possession was important in terms of spawning copycat cases of possession, in addition to fueling the anti-Huguenot frenzy engulfing France. In 1582, four individuals were publicly exorcised in the French city of Soissons. One of these, a 13-year-old child called Laurent, was said to have been possessed by a demon known as Bonsoir. Another possessed stood out because he was a 50-year-old guy who had been possessed twice (repossessed?). A third instance was even more unique since it included a lady called Marguerite Obry (not related), who claimed to be possessed by the same Beelzebub who had previously possessed Nicole Aubrey.

Though the Soissons' belongings were never as well-known as Nicole Aubry's, there were many parallels. When holy relics were placed on their stomachs or forced to drink holy water, all possessions fell into convulsions. They also charged the local Huguenots with numerous religious offences, as Nicole Aubrey did. The demons allegedly claimed to have come to "comfort their Huguenot pals" but were compelled to acknowledge the might of the True Church during the public Exorcism that drove them away.

After hearing about Nicole Aubrey's case, Marthe Brossier, the last famous possession case of the 16th century, allegedly became convinced that she was possessed. Marthe's family transported her from town to town in the Loire valley beginning in 1598, when she had several public exorcisms. This went on for nearly a year before French officials detained her for fear of inciting anti-Huguenot hatred. Marthe either fled (or was assisted in escaping) and resumed her search for exorcisms, this time in southern France. Despite her trip to Rome and appeals to the Vatican, Marthe was diagnosed with sickness rather than being possessed.

Though the period of possession was far from finished, the Nicole Aubrey exorcism and others like it became a major plank in the Catholic Church's propaganda battle against Protestant movements. The "miracle of Laon" would live on in Catholic tradition long after the political upheaval that inspired it had subsided. The fact that Exorcism and incidents of demonic possession are still practised in many countries today indicates its usefulness as a technique for bolstering belief systems challenged by criticism. The effectiveness of that technique is determined by people's willingness to believe the unbelievable.

12. Elizabeth Knapp (The Groton Witch)

Elizabeth Knapp was born in 1655 in Massachusetts. When she was 16, she worked as a servant for Reverend Samuel Willard of Groton, Massachusetts, when she began to show indications of being possessed by the Devil.

Reverend Willard noticed that when her symptoms worsened – she had severe fits, complained of being strangled, and attempted to hurl herself into the fire. She began to "carry herself in a weird and unwelcome manner," saw apparitions and had violent "fits" for three months.

During one of her fits, she talked in a "hollow" voice and referred to the minister as "a huge black rogue" who "tell[s] the people a company of falsehoods." "Satan, thou are a liar and a deceiver, and God will vindicate His truth one day," Willard said. Others in the room joined in the fight, informing the Devil that "God had him in chains."

The response was, "For all my chain, I can hit thee in the head whenever I choose." Meanwhile, Elizabeth said that the Devil had promised to turn her into a "witch" if she signed a "contract" to become his servant in her voice.

Events in Groton proceeded on the idea that Satan entices some individuals to enter into a contract with him, assuring them, as he told Elizabeth Knapp, that everything "shall be fine." They no longer have to be concerned about sin and salvation. The inhabitants of Groton likewise believed that good would triumph over evil in the whole course of God's providence.

As the tale of Elizabeth Knapp illustrates, certain difficulties sprang from Puritanism's religious demands. One expectation was that Christians perform their moral obligations to the best of their abilities. Another need was that people analyze their reasons to see whether they had adequately repented of sin and placed their whole confidence in Christ's compassion.

Reverend Willard's

Elizabeth respected the guy who served as both her Priest and her master when she wasn't possessed. When the demons were in her, though, she was vehemently opposed to him. She screamed at him, calling him a liar. She chastised her father and others for paying attention to him; questioned his authority in society and his control over her.

She had reason to dislike him. He was a young, well-off, Harvard-educated clergyman with a promising future. She was a young lady with little education and minor prospects other than servitude to others, whether as a servant, a daughter, or a wife.

He spent most of his free time reading, writing, and travelling. She had never been taught to write, seldom left Groton, and spent her time washing his house, caring for his children, bringing in his wood, and keeping his fires going - all so he could work in peace and comfort.

Puritan America was not the only place where witches were hunted. It happened in both Catholic and Protestant sections of Europe, and the toll in New England was considerably lower than in Scotland or portions of France and Germany. It's unclear why witch-hunting became lethal in certain

Puritan villages but not others. Elizabeth Knapp was not a witch in any way. She married Samuel Scripture and lived a nice Puritan wife and mother's life. She was so adept at erasing her dissatisfaction that she nearly totally vanishes from public records after 1673.

Conclusion:

The answer to the forever question, "Is the paranormal real or just fiction?" hasn't been more obvious as many strange things happen around us all the time; things that, to the ordinary eye, one would say are impossible or absurd. For example, if you look at the ordeals, the Smurls had to go through, that alone is enough to stamp a big "No" on any thoughts of relocating to a house with an unknown history or origins, but almost every day, people are migrating to new unknown locations. Furthermore, what of the cases of demonic possessions misdiagnosed as mental illness? In the world today, the contents of the medical thesaurus about diseases and other forms of illnesses keep growing, and it has reached a stage where there is hardly an ailment that doesn't have a medical term ascribed to it.

On the issue of Exorcism, though, I find it quite disturbing that very few victims of demonic possessions survive the process. The whole point of finding a cure or solution for misfortune is not to die during the treatment process or right after. The essence of the whole process is to survive the treatment process, get well, and move on with life. Anything different only states the obvious that the remedy didn't work or that the tendency to live through an exorcism and come out on top is very slim. If that's the case, then it'll be easy to stick to an incurable medical term. But then, I guess the demons won't leave without putting up a fight with the host and exorcist, and since we all are different, there is no exact point that we can use as a threshold for how much pressure and torment all humans can withstand. The exorcists may not know the extent to which they are to push the body, and if that limit is exceeded, then more often than not, it leads to a sad ending that takes us to the next issue.

The deaths of the demon-possessed victims are always pinned on the exorcists and their assistants. It's almost like a trend following the victim's death and more like an avenue for people who have contradicting beliefs to devour the accused. Like any other frontline worker, they are tasked with controlling the incidence or spread of demonic possessions, which by now should be convincing to anyone in prior disbelief of its existence. These exorcists should receive accolades for volunteering to do the dirty work of freeing souls tormented here on earth because the victims, as much as we can blame the demons, can be the sources of their predicaments. While some victims are innocent and unfortunately get pulled into some circumstances, some people purposely didn't let their sleeping dogs lie by looking for these demons from some discoveries or research or ignorantly participating in rituals that provoked the deities or demons. So, if you look at it, some of the exorcists get unfair treatment because doctors don't get arrested and dragged to court for a surgery gone wrong, so why should exorcists be punished for helping to get rid of angry, stubborn demons.

Printed in Great Britain
by Amazon

d82d1d19-2fa5-4c43-85c9-095874b9ec9eR01